FIELD GUIDE
TO
NEIGHBORHOOD
OUTREACH

ideas

Group

Loveland, Colorado

www.group.com

Group resources actually work!

This Group resource incorporates our R.E.A.L. approach to ministry. It reinforces a growing friendship with Jesus, encourages long-term learning, and results in life transformation, because it's

Relational
Learner-to-learner interaction enhances learning and builds Christian friendships.

Experiential
What learners experience through discussion and action sticks with them up to 9 times longer than what they simply hear or read.

Applicable
The aim of Christian education is to equip learners to be both hearers and doers of God's Word.

Learner-based
Learners understand and retain more when the learning process takes into consideration how they learn best.

Field Guide to Neighborhood Outreach
Copyright © 2007 Group Publishing, Inc.

Visit our Web site: www.group.com

Credits
Contributors: Heather Dunn, Cheri Gillard, Gina Leuthauser, James Miller, Jim Misloski, Summer Salomonsen, Susan Tripp, Michael van Schooneveld, and Vicki L. Witte
Chief Creative Officer: Joani Schultz
Senior Developer: Roxanne Wieman
Acquisitions Editor: Jan Kershner
Editor: Kelli B. Trujillo
Assistant Editor: Dena Twinem
Print Production Artist: Andrea Boven Nelson
Cover Art Director: Jeff A. Storm
Cover Illustrator: Andrea Boven Nelson
Cover Designer: Jeff A. Storm
Illustrator: Jeff A. Storm
Production Manager: DeAnne Lear

Unless otherwise indicated, all Scripture quotations are taken from the *Holy Bible*, New Living Translation, copyright © 1996, 2004. Used by permission of Tyndale House Publishers, Inc., Carol Stream, Illinois 60188. All rights reserved.

Library of Congress Cataloging-in-Publication Data
Field guide to neighborhood outreach. -- 1st American pbk. ed.
    p. cm.
  Includes index.
  ISBN-13: 978-0-7644-3589-8 (pbk. : alk. paper)
  1. Evangelistic work. 2. Church work. 3. Neighborhood. I. Group Publishing.
  BV3790.F46 2007
  269'.2--dc22

                    2007016367

ISBN 978-0-7644-3589-8
0-7644-3181-1

10 9 8 7 6 5 4 3 2   16 15 14 13 12 11 10 09 08
Printed in the United States of America.

TABLE OF CONTENTS

INTRODUCTION   5

HOW TO REACH OUT TO YOUR NEIGHBORHOOD   7

CREATING A CARING COMMUNITY

A "Best Of" Guide	18	Moving Day	33
Bright Bulbs	19	Neighborhood Bicycle Exchange	35
Calling All Hands!	20	Neighborhood Cleanup	36
Clothing Exchange	22	Neighborhood Garage Sale	37
Community Carnival	23	Neighborhood Mapping	38
Community Pancake Breakfast	24	Neighborhood Watch	40
Create a Social Pool With a Car Pool	25	Pack up the Van	41
Encourage 'Em	27	Parenting Seminar	43
Furniture Fix	28	Pen Pals and Flower Pots	44
Helping Kids Excel	29	Serving Single Parents	46
A Little Relief	30	Swap Meet and Greet	47
Making It Easy to "Do Good"	31	Welcome to the Neighborhood	49

EATING TOGETHER: FOOD-RELATED OUTREACH IDEAS

Bakery Barter Bonanza	52	Neighborhood Cooking Class	63
Blast From Your Past Potluck	53	Progressive Dinner Party	65
Bread Exchange	54	Recipe Rally	67
Community Mystery Dinner	56	Salsa Smackdown	69
Dinner Around the World	58	Share a CSA Share	71
Dinner by Design	60	Soup Swap	72
Eat Meat Club	61	Super Supper Club	74
Finals Food...and More	62	Ultimate Tasting Party	75

Sports and Outdoor Fun

Computer Game Tournament	78
Exercise Buddies	79
Flag Football	80
Flower Bulb and Seed Swap	82
Neighborhood Baseball	83
Neighborhood Camp Out	84
Neighborhood Splash Day	85
Neighborhood Vegetable Garden Co-op	86
Sledding Social	87
Shooting in the Breeze	88
Street Hockey	89
Tandem Dog Walking	90

Indoor Fun and Friendship

All About the Academy Awards	92
Block Book Club	93
Board Game Bash	94
Bunco	96
Finale Night Party	98
Lovely Ladies Tea Party	100
Make the Most of Movie Nights	102
Money Matters	104
Movie Night	105
Movie 1	107
Movie 2	108
Movie 3	109
Movie 4	110
Movie 5	111
Movie 6	112
NASCAR Race Day	113
Neighborhood Craft Night	114
Pamper Yourself Party	115
Seekers' Study	116
Senior Story Source	117
Tournament-Style Fun	118
Weekly Watch	119
Women Encouragement Partners	121

Holidays and Seasonal Celebrations

Autumn Festival	124
Christmas Tea	125
Christmas Wrap-Up	126
Easter-Egg Hunt	127
Gingerbread Houses	128
Halloween Alternative	130
Halloween Handouts	131
Light up Your Neighborhood	132
May Day Baskets	133
Mother's Day Dinner	134
National Night Out	135
Neighborhood Parade	137
Patriotic Pet Parade	139
Super Bowl Party	140
Vibrant Valentine	141

Index	143

INTRODUCTION

It's easy to go through weeks, months, or even years without ever meeting our neighbors. We can drive right into our garages and walk straight into our homes without ever seeing or building relationships with those around us. But God calls us to break free from that isolated way of living that is so prevalent in our culture. God wants you to be a light in your neighborhood!

Field Guide to Neighborhood Outreach will equip you with a variety of fun, creative, and exciting ways you can meet your neighbors and build meaningful relationships with them. And as you develop authentic caring friendships, you'll have opportunities to share Christ's love through words and actions.

The first step toward developing those friendships is to meet your neighbors. And yeah, we know it can feel a little cheesy to just ring a doorbell and say, "Hi, I'm your neighbor!" So in **"How to Reach Out to Your Neighborhood,"** we've included a step-by-step guide from a couple who has already forged new territory in neighborhood outreach. Their inspiring story will inspire you to take to your streets!

Then we give you the nuts and bolts ideas to use in *your* neighborhood with *your* neighbors! In **"Creating a Caring Community,"** you'll find suggestions and ideas for fun and easy ways to meet and interact with your neighbors by caring for each other and fostering an authentic sense of community where you live.

Gathering around an outdoor barbecue is a natural way for neighbors to interact. In **"Eating Together: Food-Related Outreach Ideas,"** you'll find mouth-watering ideas for parties and themed get-togethers that go beyond the backyard cookout and create memories your community will treasure.

"Sports and Outdoor Fun" and **"Indoor Fun and Friendship"** are two sections you don't want to miss, jampacked with suggestions for gatherings and events that will be filled with laughter, smiles, and deepening friendships.

And what better time to gather together with neighbors than during traditional **"Holidays and Seasonal Celebrations"**! Here, you'll discover holidays with a twist—fun ways of celebrating traditions that involve your neighbors.

And look for the Helpful Hints and Instant Intentions sections. Helpful Hints are just that—tips or trivia to make your idea just a little bit better. And Instant Intentions offer ways to take the next step in helping your neighbor know Jesus.

God has planted you right where you live for a purpose. Let your light shine!

HOW TO REACH OUT TO YOUR NEIGHBORHOOD

This man and wife single-handedly built a sense of community by reaching out to everyone in their neighborhood. What can you learn from their example?

THE EVOLUTION OF THE IDEA

The neighborhood outreach ministry of Drue and Laura Warner began before they even moved into their neighborhood. As Laura explains, "My thinking on neighborhood ministry was really solidified after reading *Making Room for Life* by Randy Frazee. We read it as we were looking for a house to buy, and we had really been praying that God would lead us to the place he had prepared."

Drue adds, "We know we probably can't affect the entire city of Atlanta, but we may be able to impact our neighborhood and potentially even the suburb of Sugar Hill, where we live."

Laura and Drue say their hearts are in alignment with the ministry vision of their church, Perimeter Church, in Duluth, Georgia. According to Drue, the church's vision is "to bring the people of greater Atlanta and all places we serve into a life-transforming encounter with the kingdom of God." He continues, "We believe that one of the greatest tools the church has today to accomplish such a mission is serving and loving others, particularly those with special physical or emotional needs."

As a result of that vision, Drue and Laura made a decision. "Since we're both extroverts and gifted with hospitality and mercy," explains Drue, "the best use of our time with the greatest potential for spiritual fruit in the lives of others is to focus our efforts on meeting, building relationships with, and serving our neighbors and local public elementary school."

THE HEART OF THE MINISTRY

The couple moved into Lenox Park, a neighborhood of 240 homes, in August 2004. They wasted no time beginning their ministry. "Our first effort to begin meeting neighbors and building relationships was to coordinate a neighborhood food drive in October 2004," says Drue.

It was important not to collect food door-to-door, but rather to have a central drop-off location. This gave neighbors the opportunity to stop by, have coffee and doughnuts, and meet one another. Drue and Laura also had a sign-up sheet available for neighbors who were interested in building a greater sense of community in the neighborhood. Ten people signed up.

After explaining their vision for community service and neighborhood relationships at the next homeowners' meeting, 15 more people signed up. And the ministry grew wings.

OTHER OUTREACH OPPORTUNITIES

The couple began hosting Saturday morning breakfast gatherings for neighbors who expressed interest in building a greater sense of community. At these breakfast gatherings, the group cast its vision for more outreach ideas, and Laura and Drue helped the group come up with ideas of how to implement its intentions.

The result? The neighborhood has held a tsunami-relief drive, a summer pool party, an Easter-egg hunt, and a holiday decorating contest. In addition, 200 people attended a Halloween "meet and greet."

Drue even dressed up as Santa for the neighborhood kids. "I was asked to be Santa Claus for a Christmas party for foster and adopted children through Bethany Christian Services," he explains. "I figured while I had the suit, we could go ahead and use it as a relational ministry tool and invite neighborhood families to bring the kids over to our house to see Santa." In addition, Laura and "Santa" gave families a news article that directed them toward the spiritual significance of Christmas.

The couple also hosted a caroling party one year. They invited neighbors who had been involved in many of their other activities throughout the year, and almost 20 people participated. Laura says, "Ages ranged from retired people, young couples, singles, and families with kids. The diversity in age added a richness and sense of real community to the group, and that was a blessing."

A further blessing, she says, was the response to the caroling. The recipients, whom Drue and Laura had carefully chosen, included a wife (with two children) whose husband had been killed in an accident the first week of that December, an elderly woman who had placed her husband with Alzheimer's disease in a nursing home the previous summer, a widow whose husband had died on Christmas day two years earlier, and several people who had just moved into the neighborhood.

"There was such a combination of tears and laughter along the way," recalls Laura. "We had a very rich, wonderful time together."

One of their most recent outreach ideas is a campaign to read through the Bible. The couple also plans to open their home one Sunday night a month so people can come over to discuss spiritual issues. "We have no idea how this is going to go," says Laura, "but we feel that the time is right."

> "All it takes is stepping out. Our community, our country is ready for it."
> **DRUE WARNER, *Community Outreach Associate, Perimeter Church, Duluth, Georgia***

BUILDING RELATIONSHIPS

At this writing, Drue can readily count off ways that this neighborhood outreach ministry has built solid relationships that might never have developed otherwise.

- Out of 240 homes, the Warners have built relationships with more than 75 neighbors and have developed close relationships with 20 of them.
- The neighborhood has donated more than 100 bags of groceries in the first two years of the ministry, building a firm sense of community among the donors.
- The Warners have identified deep emotional needs in four of their

neighbors—needs that otherwise would never have been known.

- Four families have expressed interest in attending or have attended church with Drue and Laura.
- Two men have attended Perimeter's annual men's retreat.
- Laura and Drue have had conversations about spiritual issues with 12 families.
- Six to eight couples have expressed interest in starting a small group that would focus on marriage and family issues.

None of these things would have happened without the intentional outreach of Laura and Drue. "Think about our culture. At least in suburban Atlanta, we are very busy, scattered, disconnected people," says Laura. "When you get together with friends, it is typically to meet at a restaurant or go to some other activity. It is rare to spend time in someone else's home. But there the experience is much richer."

"We view our home as a primary tool for ministry."

LAURA WARNER

SHARING THE GOSPEL

There are many ways to share the gospel, and certainly not all of those ways are oral. "We've shared the gospel through Christmas cards," says Drue, "and by including our neighbors in e-mails and prayer requests when we learned during Laura's pregnancy that our daughter had a heart defect."

Laura and Drue share the gospel by their actions more than their words. "We've been intentional about not verbally sharing our faith— that is, evangelizing—with our neighbors or inviting them to church events until we've built a foundation of trust and respect," explains Drue. "We don't want to be perceived as having an agenda of trying to convert them or get them to come to our church." After relationships have been forged, however, Drue says they are able to share the gospel freely because of the mutual trust they've established.

They strive to show their neighbors unconditional love and acceptance, rather than judging them. The couple wants to serve their neighbors with an attitude of humility, love, and acceptance.

Drue and Laura intentionally connect on a regular basis with other Christians they've met in the neighborhood. Together, they cast vision for the neighborhood outreach and pray together for their non-Christian neighbors.

Those efforts have paid great dividends. "I'd say that about 75 neighbors have experienced and/or heard the gospel through our neighborhood ministry," says Drue." The relationships we're building will give us a great avenue for sharing the gospel—in our lives and in our words."

DAY-TO-DAY OUTREACH

Their neighborhood outreach hasn't cost Laura and Drue much in terms of dollars. "There's been a small financial cost to us," says Laura. "We often end up feeding others," she laughs. But since they piggyback on many of the events already planned and paid for within the subdivision, their costs are minimal, according to Drue.

Those events include pool parties, summer cookouts, and other social events planned and paid for by the homeowners' association. "We tap into those events," says Drue. "We make it a point to attend, meet new people, and deepen existing friendships."

"We make sure that we are volunteering, participating, and mingling with neighbors during these events," adds Laura.

Laura and Drue are intentional about giving their contact information to neighbors they meet for the first time. "We want them to have an opportunity to connect with us," explains Drue. "We typically don't ask for phone numbers, but we do try to find out where people live so we can stop by for a quick visit while out for an afternoon walk."

In addition, the couple serves the homeowners' association board as welcome team coordinators. The board sends them the names and addresses of people who have just moved into the neighborhood. "We try to make personal visits, delivering a current neighborhood newsletter and typically some cookies," Laura explains. Many of those first meetings result in further interaction, such as borrowing yard tools or asking for job contacts and school recommendations.

Other times, the couple invites new neighbors to dinner to meet established members of the neighborhood. "That way we're not the only contacts people have," Laura says. "We try to match newlyweds with other young couples, families with kids of the same age, and so on." At this writing, Laura and Drue plan to start a Saturday morning coffee gathering to which they'll invite both old and new neighbors.

THE COST OF THE CALLING

The cost is more in terms of time, but it's a cost both Laura and Drue are willing to pay. "We've installed a glass storm door, so the main front door is almost always open," explains Laura. "In fact, typically we close the main front door around 9 p.m., and we joke about being closed for business."

All joking aside, the glass storm door serves a very practical purpose. "Many of our neighbors know that if the main door is open, meaning that you can see into the house and the porch light is on, visitors are welcome." Otherwise, she says, the family is enjoying personal time. "We tell people about our open/closed-door policy."

To preserve family time and avoid burnout, the couple generally keeps the door closed early in the morning as they enjoy breakfast together, and again in the evening during their daughter's bath and bedtime. In addition, Drue's responsibilities at the church often allow him to work at home half days on Fridays, during which time the door stays closed. The couple also values time away, making sure that family retreats are part of their annual calendar.

The couple has built enough relationships with neighbors, says Laura, "that barely a day goes by that someone doesn't stop by for a short or long visit." Someone might stop by to borrow a spice; someone else might need a listening ear.

To make the ministry vital and viable, Drue and Laura have to be willing to surrender their time and to-do lists to be available to their neighbors. "Many Saturday projects get put on the back burner," says Laura, "not to mention the countless times I've just put the unfolded laundry

"Many of our neighbors have become true friends. It's nice to be able to see them often and not have to drive and battle traffic."

LAURA WARNER

back in the basket to make room for a neighbor on the sofa.'"

When household jobs simply have to be done, Laura says, "We'll talk to neighbors as we work—or invite them to join us! We just tell people we have to keep working when that's appropriate to the situation."

The ministry has also required a bit of personal sacrifice for the couple. In an intentional effort to spend more time at home, Laura hasn't been able to dive into all of the women's ministry activities she's interested in at church. "We've cut out other things in our schedule in order to spend more time with neighbors," agrees Drue, "things like taking time off from a church discipleship group in order to try to develop a group within our neighborhood." But both agree the extra effort is worthwhile.

"People are hungry for a sense of community, but nobody knows what to do. It just takes somebody to stand up and say, 'Let's do something!'"

DRUE WARNER

"We want to be available to share our lives with the people God has placed around us," Laura says, "and that is key to this ministry."

BEARING FRUIT

Are Drue and Laura pleased with the fruit of this young ministry? Most definitely!

"In one way or another," says Drue, "this outreach has affected every neighbor (approximately 500 people) in our 240-home subdivision." If for no other reason, that impact has come about because Drue and Laura were instrumental in restarting the neighborhood newsletter. "Through communication comes influence," chuckles Drue.

When asked to sum up their neighborhood outreach ministry, Drue answers, "I would characterize this as a seed-planting, relationship-building, long-term ministry. Our goal is to be continually planting seeds of the love of Christ as we seek to establish and deepen relationships over the long haul."

The outreach has certainly been instrumental, says Drue, in building community both in his own church and in his neighborhood. "Our great passion," he says, "is to see followers of Jesus Christ who live within our own neighborhood begin to function as the body—not as members of various churches (while still maintaining active involvement there)—but as members of 'The Church of Lenox Park.'"

How to Get Started in *Your* Neighborhood

According to Drue, the idea of "loving your neighbor" is transferable from church to church, no matter what the size. "This model works best in subdivisions, dormitories, and condominium complexes," he says. "It's probably more challenging in a rural setting. However, there may be some great benefits in a rural setting because you'd have fewer neighbors and would be able to spend more time with them."

> "People don't need to go to church to experience the church."
>
> **DRUE WARNER**

If you'd like to reach out to your neighbors, heed this advice from Drue and Laura:

1. Pray. Ask God how he wants you to use your spiritual gifts, passions, and talents to minister to your neighbors.
2. Determine exactly who you will try to reach with the gospel. Set geographic boundaries—will you try to reach the people who live on your street? your block? your subdivision?
3. Brainstorm creative ways to connect with your neighbors. This can be as simple as delivering a plate of cookies to new neighbors or new parents.
4. Once you've connected with your neighbors, invite them to serve the community with you.
5. Rearrange your calendar so you can invest lots of time "in the field" (at home).
6. Be sure that all of your planning takes children into account. If their children aren't well-fed and cared for, single moms won't be drawn to this outreach.
7. Make service, love, and relationship-building your top priorities in interacting with your neighbors.
8. Wait for God's timing before you begin to verbalize your faith, all the while praying for God to open doors of opportunity and to be working in the hearts of your neighbors.

9. Be proactive in spending time with both Christian and non-Christian neighbors.
10. Discover which methods of communication seem acceptable (and unacceptable) within your neighborhood.
11. Invite and empower others in the neighborhood to get involved in the ministry.
12. Meet people exactly where they are before thinking of inviting them to attend a church function. Cautions Drue, "Motives can easily be misunderstood among non-Christians."

PLANNING A FOOD DRIVE

idea A neighborhood food drive is a good way to begin your neighborhood outreach ministry. Here are several easy steps to take in organizing an effective food drive.

- At least three weeks prior to the drive, get approval from your homeowners' association or apartment manager, if applicable.
- Two to three weeks before your drive, contact your local food bank to learn its needs, and arrange a time to deliver your neighborhood's donations.
- One to two weeks before the drive, notify your neighbors of the plan, detailing the items needed, the date, and the time of the drive. Do this by distributing a letter to each neighbor within your established boundaries.
- One week before the drive, place yard signs throughout your neighborhood.
- On the day of the drive, set up a visible drop-off location in your neighborhood. You may want to use a tent. Supply coffee, doughnuts, and information about the organization that will be receiving the food.
- Provide a sign-up sheet to collect neighbors' contact information.
- Also ask neighbors to indicate if they'd be interested in future neighborhood outreach projects.
- Within one week of the drive, deliver the donations.
- Optional: After the drive, connect with neighbors who participated. Serve refreshments at your house, or plan a cookout to say thanks.

"*Love your neighbor as yourself.*"

LEVITICUS 19:18B

CREATING A
CARING COMMUNITY

"Dear children, let's not merely say that we love each other; let us show the truth by our actions. Our actions will show that we belong to the truth, so we will be confident when we stand before God."

1 JOHN 3:18-19

A caring community is a safe, friendly place to live. It's a place where neighbors reach out to one another, help one another, laugh with one another. It's a place we all want to live.

You can create such a place in your own community. Use the ideas in this chapter to forge lasting relationships with those neighbors next door, across the street, and down the block.

Show Jesus' love to your neighbors by the things you say and do.

A "BEST OF" GUIDE

idea Enlist your neighbors in the search for the best of everything—or at least the most important things.

Make a list of helpful as well as fun things you and your neighbors would enjoy. Include things like parks, doctors, dentists, dry cleaners, fast-food restaurants, date-night restaurants, electronics companies, hairdressers, auto repair places, coffee houses, day cares, churches, and so on. Make the list into a table for your neighbors to fill in so you can get the address, phone number, Web site, and any other pertinent information for each of the places they recommend.

> **HELPFUL HINTS**
> Contact your "Best Of" winners to let them know they've been noticed. They may want to offer a coupon or flier for you to include in your directory.

Distribute the list, along with an explanatory note, to all of your neighbors. In your note, introduce yourself; explain your motivation; tell them to cast votes for their favorites by writing in the name and address of a business in each category. Explain when you'll need their votes and when they'll get the results. Send a reminder several days before your deadline, or host a simple coffee or dessert at your place so that people can drop off their votes and actually see the tallying.

Tally the results, and make copies for everyone. Don't worry about being fancy. A staple in the corner and a bold title is good enough— though you could make a creative book if you're so inclined. Just be sure to deliver it when you promised!

Instant Intentions

Distribute your "Best Of" directories personally, and thank each neighbor for participating. Keep several extra copies to hand to new neighbors as a welcome-to-the-neighborhood gift.

BRIGHT BULBS

idea Do you ever find yourself waving to that semi-familiar-looking family down the street…but you've never actually taken the time to introduce yourself?

Use this idea to make your community safer and brighter—and get to know the people you live near but may not often interact with. A great time to perform this service is at the beginning of spring after the long, dark winter nights have left many outside lights extinguished.

You can do this activity solo, with your family, or with a group of neighbors. Arm each person with several boxes of fresh light bulbs, empty plastic bags or boxes to hold burnt-out bulbs, and a pair of lightweight gloves to use while handling hot bulbs. Make sure to carry light bulbs of varying wattages to cover different models of lighting fixtures.

Then walk your neighborhood streets, approaching each resident one by one and offering to replace burnt-out light

> **HELPFUL HINTS**
> *Don't be surprised if some of the people you meet ask if you could replace light bulbs inside, too! Perhaps an elderly person just can't get up to the attic to replace a bulb. Have extra bulbs on hand, or offer to come back at a later time to help.*

bulbs on their porch or driveway. At each door, present the friendly explanation of a chance to introduce yourselves, as well as the benefits of brighter streets (such as increased safety) in your community. If a home's porch lights aren't visibly extinguished, stop to offer your services anyway—don't miss the opportunity to say hello to a neighbor…besides, perhaps their *back* porch light is burnt out!

Instant Intentions

Keep a small notebook with you, and after leaving a house, discreetly write the names, address, and any information you learned from the neighbors you just met. That way, the next time you meet, you'll be able to greet them by name and ask how Jimmy's baseball game went. It's those little things that can mean the most in forming a closer relationship.

CALLING ALL HANDS!

idea Here's a way to find the help you need from the teenagers in your area while inspiring their entrepreneurial spirit: Set up a basic teenage job directory for your neighborhood.

This is a simple way to connect willing teens with neighbors who would like to hire temporary work. Begin by preparing a blank master list with several sections for name, age, phone number or e-mail address, interests (pet-sitting, yardwork, babysitting), skills (first-aid- or CPR-certified), and any other categories you think would be appropriate for your area. Go door to door, and ask teenagers if they'd like to take part in the job listing. Make sure you obtain their parents' permission for them to be included on the list. Also give teenagers your name and contact information in case they need to update their status or interests on the list.

HELPFUL HINTS

Encourage those who are interested in babysitting to take a first-aid or CPR certification class, and provide them with information about these classes. This will not only inspire more confidence in the parents who are looking for sitters, but will also help to improve general neighborhood first-aid and safety awareness—one person at a time.

If you have a neighborhood news-letter, request to make the job directory a monthly feature, and update it frequently. If you have a neighborhood Web site or e-mail service, submit this list to be posted there (look into password protection so as not to broadcast the sensitive information of minors). It's also a nice touch to hand out a hard copy of the information to your neighbors so they have quick access to the new directory.

You could also consider adding a section for neighbors to post a memo with a specific job that they're looking for help with, such as painting a shed, and give teens the opportunity to respond directly to the requests.

Follow up with teenagers and neighbors who are part of your list, checking on how their experiences have been. Seriously consider and implement all helpful suggestions to your system. Make sure to hire some of the teenagers on the list to help in your own household, and pay them generously.

CLOTHING EXCHANGE

idea Spring cleaning is never fun, especially going through kids' closets and getting rid of clothes that no longer fit. Did you ever think of reaching your neighbors through your kids' outgrown clothing? Well, you can with a clothing exchange!

Send out a flier announcing to your neighbors that you are going to be holding a clothing exchange. Begin with children's clothes and shoes. If it's a success and neighbors show interest, include toys, books, and games in your next exchange.

Have large blankets spread out on your grass and large tables to display items. Also have plenty of empty hangers and places to hang clothing. Rope tied between two trees or ladders works well. As neighbors arrive, assist them in displaying their items.

HELPFUL HINTS

To make the exchange fair, before beginning, give everyone one ticket for each item they are bringing to the exchange. When they have made their selections, they can "buy" their items with their tickets. If a person ends up with extra tickets, he or she can either donate them to someone else or save them for the next exchange.

Remember, this is an exchange, not using money, but clothes. No money should ever be involved. Make that clear to your neighbors before you begin.

Instant Intentions

Invite some of your neighbors to stay for lunch after the exchange. Over lunch, talk about what a blessing it is to have neighbors you can share clothes with and how good God is to provide in that way.

COMMUNITY CARNIVAL

idea Kids of all ages love carnivals. From the ringtoss to the cakewalk, the dunking machine to the pony rides, there's something for everyone!

Put on a carnival for the whole neighborhood. Have it in your front yard or in a neighborhood park (get permission first, if necessary).

Snacks such as bags of popcorn, candy, huge hot pretzels, cotton candy, and snow cones are always welcomed treats. Machines can be rented to make carnival treats, or you can create and use your own setup.

Rented blow-up bouncers are always a hit, if your budget allows. Low-cost attractions might include a miniature or Frisbee golf course, squirt-gun tag games, outdoor bowling, a water-balloon toss, a giant bubble maker, and the age-and-weight-guessing game.

Roaming entertainers will add to the fun. Recruit closet magicians or clowns from your neighborhood to join the fun. Musicians will be sure to please,

> **HELPFUL HINTS**
> *Make sure all your neighbors know they are welcome. Advertise the event with fliers and posters, or deliver invitations to each house. Use the opportunity to enjoy some good, old-fashioned fun with your neighbors!*

whether they provide concerts or wandering entertainment. Strolling singers can add a laugh by singing requests or changing lyrics on the spot to fit a situation.

Let the day culminate with an evening cookout.

Instant Intentions

As you advertise the event, especially if you go door to door, don't be afraid to ask for help with the carnival. Explain that you're trying to create a sense of community in your neighborhood, and you can use all the help you can get! Have a list of jobs available for people to choose from, and have a planning party at your house.

COMMUNITY PANCAKE BREAKFAST

idea A pancake breakfast is a relatively easy and inexpensive way to bring your neighborhood together. (Who doesn't like free food?)

Join with one or two other neighbors to plan the event. If your neighborhood has a community building, get permission to use it on the specified Saturday morning. If not, have the breakfast in a local park or even in your driveway if you get a lot of traffic going by.

Then get the word out in your community—for example, distribute fliers, post signs, or use old-fashioned word of mouth. Highlight that this is a free event for anyone who wants to come and meet and visit with his or her neighbors.

> **HELPFUL HINTS**
> *Have a community building sign-up sheet available for neighbors who would like to continue getting to know each other; then get together to plan future events for your neighborhood.*

The affair can be as simple or as extravagant as you wish. For a simple pancake breakfast, all you'll need are some boxes of pancake mix, large bowls, water, skillets, metal spatulas, ladles, and a heat source. If you can't use a community kitchen, set up tables and plug in electric skillets in your driveway or at your local park. Have paper plates, plastic forks, napkins, and syrup for your hungry guests.

This event offers an opportunity for people in your community to get to know each other. It can be done on a monthly or quarterly basis, depending on the response.

Instant Intentions

As people gather before the breakfast, start the event with a short prayer of thanksgiving for the people in your neighborhood. Be ready to explain that you wanted to have the breakfast to show how thankful you are to God for your neighbors.

CREATE A SOCIAL POOL
WITH A CAR POOL

idea Set up a ride share contact list for your neighborhood. This idea is perfect for environmentally conscious people who would love to save gasoline while making some new social contacts.

A list such as this will work best if posted on your neighborhood Web site or electronic forum. Or, create a list, photocopy it, and distribute it to your neighbors.

Create three sections within your car-pool topic: "Commuters wishing to share driving," "Commuters looking for rides," and "Car pools looking for riders." Create an instruction page that helps people know what type of information they should post in each category. For instance, have people specify the dates they are available, commute times (both length and what time they need to arrive or leave a

> **HELPFUL HINTS**
> *Also include a section on your list with pertinent information such as "non-smoker" or "dogs ride in car" in case someone has an allergy. Offer a way for ride-share participants to provide you with feedback on the process and the outcome of their carpooling.*

certain location), origin and end points of their commute, and how many seats are available in their vehicle. And of course, have people post their phone numbers or e-mail addresses so they can contact one another to arrange the rides. For ease of use, you could even set up a chart or spreadsheet that can be filled in with the proper information, and then users can access the data they need in an easy-to-read grid format.

This car-pool list doesn't have to be used just for those commuting to and from work. It could also be a great place to connect with people traveling to major events around town (such as a sporting event or local fair), or even for youth and young adults to find ride shares to and from school.

Advertise the details of your car-pool listing by posting fliers around your neighborhood or by sending out a neighborhood e-mail. And then start taking advantage of shared rides with your neighbors!

Instant Intentions

Traveling with people you don't know very well can be exciting, but it can also be awkward. Be prepared in advance with some questions and conversation starters to get the ball rolling. Absorb the new information you're learning about your neighbors, and then if you share rides in the future you can bring up a familiar topic, or ask them about something you learned the last time you rode together. If the opportunity arises, ask a car pool partner if you can pray for a certain situation in his or her life—and then follow up with the person later to see how they're doing.

ENCOURAGE 'EM

idea If you have the gift of encouragement, this will be easy for you! Be the neighbor who brings out the best in others.

Keep an eye on your neighbors—to see what they're doing well. Collect or create a variety of simple notecards. Tell the gardener how great his or her flowers look. The neighbor who faithfully walks his or her dog—and picks up after it—deserves a "thanks." Notice when neighbors help others, go out of their way to be friendly, or pick up trash.

Look for grown-ups as well as children, grandparents, and teenagers, too. Take two minutes to write a note and send or deliver it. It'll feel good to know you live in such a great neighborhood. Who knows how many blessings you'll plant, water, and even reap!

> **HELPFUL HINTS**
>
> *Here's some inspiration, direct from Scripture:* "The generous will prosper; those who refresh others will themselves be refreshed" (Proverbs 11:25).

Instant Intentions

Keep a stash of notecards in your car or by your front window. When you see something great, write it down right away. If you don't know someone's name or address, just hand it to him or her or leave the note in the person's door or under the windshield wiper of his or her car. It'll be a great way to introduce yourself.

FURNITURE FIX

idea If you've ever passed an auction or garage sale offering lots of furniture, you've probably noticed a crowd. Furniture is an often-sought-after commodity, perhaps because its function is such a basic necessity. So use the necessity of furniture as a way to meet and form relationships with your neighbors.

Scour your attic, basement, and garage. Surely there's a table you haven't used in years or a chair just begging for repair. Then ask your

HELPFUL HINTS

Dispose of any used stripping agent in a sealed container. And be careful not to sand too heavily on veneered wood— you may sand right through the veneer.

neighbors to do the same thing. You could even go to local thrift shops, garage sales, and auctions. Who knows what treasures you may find? Then get to work!

Invite your neighbors over for a day of furniture fixing! Set up a well-ventilated work area, and purchase safety wear (gloves, face masks, and goggles). A book on the basics of furniture repair is a good idea, too.

Unless you have an experienced woodworker in your group, start with small projects. Sometimes an older piece of furniture just needs a good cleaning to be functional again, and anyone can handle that!

Once you have several pieces of furniture ready for new homes, decide how you'll distribute your goods. You could trade furniture pieces with your neighbors, donate to a local charity, or have your own give-it-away neighborhood garage sale. The recipients of your hard work will remember the love you shared each time they use that piece of furniture.

Instant Intentions

While working side by side with your neighbors, take the opportunity to learn more about their interests and hobbies. By the end of the day, you should have learned enough to suggest another group-building activity to do together.

HELPING KIDS EXCEL

idea High school, with all of its pressures and the looming possibilities of what comes next, is a hard time. Kids' minds are filled with the prospects of jobs both now and in the future, important tests they'll be taking, and questions about college and what they should study. This is an excellent time to show kids that others care about them.

Many schools have some sort of resource center, with varying amounts of information and contacts for students. With a little help from the adults in your neighborhood, you can provide even more. Make *yourselves* a resource for the kids.

Get as many people as you can in your neighborhood to write a short summary of what kind of work they do or what kinds of job skills they have, along with contact information. Organize the information into a booklet to create a neighborhood resource center. If possible, create a Web version, too.

> **HELPFUL HINTS**
>
> *With college entrance exams like the SAT and ACT, kids will need help again. You can procure test-preparation books and software from Kaplan or The Princeton Review and provide them to students at a lower cost or for free.*

Kids in your neighborhood can use this resource to learn more about various occupations, find possible mentors, and participate in job shadowing experiences. This could also be used as a resource for kids to find cool summer jobs!

Next, create a college resource. As with the job booklet, ask neighbors to write informational pieces on the schools they attended and the degree programs they majored in.

Instant Intentions

Each of these resources acts as a way of connecting with neighborhood kids; it opens the door to relationships and gives an opportunity for youth to see local adults as people they can look to for help and guidance. Whenever possible, be willing to share faith experiences from your college days and professional career.

A LITTLE RELIEF

idea There are needy kids all over the world, and the kids in your neighborhood can help!

Ask the parents in your neighborhood if they'd be willing to help organize a kid-to-kid relief effort to help a children's charity of their choice. Make your project a one-time event or even a quarterly or seasonal outreach. Here are a few ideas to help you get started:

• Collect school supplies for underprivileged children.

> **HELPFUL HINTS**
>
> *If your church uses The Easy VBS® program from Group Publishing, you may already be familiar with its Operation Kid-to-Kid™ outreach. You can build from that experience to make your project a quarterly or seasonal outreach event. If your church isn't familiar with Operation Kid-to-Kid and you'd like to know more, check it out at www.ok2k.org.*

• Gather toiletry supplies for kids in impoverished or war-torn countries.
• Collect and wrap new toys to give away at Christmas.
• Buy favorite books for kids who can't afford their own. (Be sure to suggest Bibles!)
• Send teddy bears to hospitalized children.

Whatever avenue of outreach you choose, add a personal element to your project. Let the children in your neighborhood make and sign cards to accompany the gifts. Take a group snapshot to send along. (Check with parents first to obtain permission.)

Instant Intentions

Ask recipients to write back to your kids and send pictures of themselves. The more kids can get to know the needs and hearts of other children around the nation or world, the more they'll realize the need to spread the love of Jesus far and near.

MAKING IT EASY TO "DO GOOD"

idea Many of us live in neighborhoods where people do not "need" much—at least materially. This often makes it difficult to know how to serve our neighbors. And yet most people desire to do "good deeds." Unfortunately, our busyness often keeps us from ever getting to do those deeds. Here's a way to serve your neighbors by making it easy for them to do good deeds—and open the door to significant relationships.

First, identify organizations already serving the underprivileged segments of your city's population. It may be a food kitchen or a nonprofit group that provides the homeless with warm clothing. All of these organizations depend on regular donations from people who care. Contact the leaders of the organization you would like to help, and ask for the following: a list of the items they need the most, and permission to use their organization's name to start a monthly collection in your neighborhood. You might also ask if they have a brief summary of how their organization benefits the community.

> **HELPFUL HINTS**
> *Avoid simply collecting money. Your neighbors will be more willing to give food or clothing that can't be misused or misappropriated. Make sure you are willing to commit to this collection for as long as you live in the neighborhood or until you can encourage someone else to take over.*

That is all you need to get started. Meet every month on a day and time that will be easy for everyone to remember (such as the second Saturday or the third Thursday of the month). On that day, go as a group to each of your neighbors, and introduce yourself if they don't already know you. Point to your houses so they know you live in their neighborhood. Explain to them that you are collecting for specific organizations, and that each month you are going to make a trip there to deliver donated items. Ask them for permission to stop by each month at this day and time to see if they have anything they would like to donate.

Many of your neighbors may ask you to wait while they get something immediately, so make sure you allow for enough time (and carrying capacity) on your first trip around the block.

Instant Intentions

Engaging in this activity gives you an excellent opportunity to become a regular visitor in your neighbor's home. After just a few months, you'll be able to thank your neighbors for giving—and, as a way of saying thanks, ask how you can pray for them.

You will also notice that even when your neighbors don't have anything to give, they'll simply be interested in talking with you and catching up. Make sure you set aside enough time to have these conversations. These are the conversations that will help you understand where each person is spiritually and give you ample opportunity to share about your relationship with Jesus.

MOVING DAY

idea One thing we can count on in today's society is its transience. Families are always moving—whether it's a transfer or an "upward" (or "downward" move) in the same area. Young adults are also constantly on the move—to and from college, to new apartments, or as they prepare to get married and start a new life together. It's a stressful time no matter what the reason. You can be there to reduce some of the stress—as well as some of the physical load.

As soon as you see a sale sign in your neighborhood go from "for sale" to "sold," call the realtor and explain that you'd like to welcome the new owner to your neighborhood by helping with the move. Find out the date and plan accordingly.

What do you need to make this outreach a success? Volunteers! Many moves can be completed within a few hours if there are enough people helping. Find a system that works for your neighborhood: e-mail, word of mouth, sign-up sheets, or another idea. Let volunteers know the needs for each particular move as well as dates and times.

> **HELPFUL HINTS**
>
> *This idea can work in reverse, too. If a family in the neighborhood is moving away, send them off with well wishes and a lot of help! Offer to help them pack, load the truck, or clean the residence after the move. And remember, food and drinks are appreciated whether you're coming or going!*

Depending on the number of volunteers, be ready to help unload the moving truck, help entertain small children, and have snacks and drinks available during the work.

One last especially nice touch is to bring dinner to the new neighbor on the night of the move. No one feels like cooking after a move, and most people couldn't find their pots and pans if you paid them! A simple dinner—even sandwiches—will be appreciated!

Instant Intentions

Offer your new neighbors a "Best Of" list compiled by you and your neighbors. On it, reference several choices under categories such as best cleaners, best restaurant, best haircut—and don't forget best churches! As a personal touch, give your new neighbor a handwritten welcome with your name and phone number, and say that you'd love to have them as your guests for church and lunch some Sunday after they get settled.

NEIGHBORHOOD BICYCLE EXCHANGE

idea Children grow. Bicycles don't. It's that simple. Seats and handlebars can only be raised so high. And sometimes children grow quite fast, leaving a bike in fantastic condition with no one to ride it.

Ask the parents in your neighborhood to collect the used bicycles that their children have outgrown. Explain your vision for the project, and ask for their help.

Once you have the bikes, get together with other fix-it types in your neighborhood to do whatever work might be needed on the bikes. Talk to a sports store or bike shop to see if they'd be willing to donate some grease, bike chains, or other parts. Possibly, they might even donate a few hours' labor for free.

> ### HELPFUL HINTS
> *Don't be afraid to ask parents in your church, family, and other neighborhoods to donate their used bikes. The more bikes to choose from, the bigger the bike bonanza!*

Next, pick out a time and place to give away the bikes. Ideally, that place should be your home. If that doesn't work, choose a local park or common area. Advertise your bike bonanza throughout your neighborhood. Invite everyone in the neighborhood to come claim a refurbished bike!

Give any unclaimed bikes to a local shelter or organization that provides toys for families who can't afford such things.

Instant Intentions

If you come across someone who really enjoys fixing the bikes, consider forming an ongoing bike ministry with that person. (You don't have to call it a ministry.) As you work together on more bikes to give away, chances are good that you'll have opportunities to share your faith.

NEIGHBORHOOD CLEANUP

idea Trash. It's everywhere. And, more than likely, you have stood outside your front door and eyed a sandwich wrapper make its way down the street—and wondered who will pick it up. Organizing a trash cleanup is a sure way to unite your neighborhood in service and develop relationships in the process.

Grab a clipboard and a sheet of paper. Choose an upcoming Saturday or Sunday, and write the date on the top of the paper. Make two columns: one for names and one for phone numbers. Go door to door, inviting your neighbors to join you in a neighborhood cleanup. Encourage families to bring their children. Remind participants to bring plastic gloves and large trash bags for litter.

> **HELPFUL HINTS**
> *Make sure to include children in this effort. Teaching children the negative effects of littering and the importance of preserving their communities is a lesson they will remember for the rest of their lives. Encourage families to sign up together, thereby creating family time that doubles as community service.*

On the designated day, before you begin the cleanup, take a few moments to talk through some safety tips such as watching for cars, avoiding busy streets, supervising children, not picking up broken glass, and so on.

Depending on where your neighborhood is located, you may want to focus the trash pickup in a local park or community area, side streets, or alleyways.

Instant Intentions

When neighborhood cleanup is finished, invite the participants to your home for some refreshments. Talk about the neighborhood, ask how long each family has been there, what their best memories are, and what they have seen change; and listen to what they say. This information will provide you with an "in" for developing further contact.

NEIGHBORHOOD GARAGE SALE

idea Use the power of numbers to bring in the crowds and sell, sell, sell! Organize a neighborhood garage sale. Contact each neighbor in person or with a flier describing the sale, dates and times, and offering suggestions. State in the flier that, on the day of the sale, a small dollar amount will be collected from each participant to cover the cost of a newspaper ad. Or, you can collect a set amount ahead of time and use any excess to purchase supplies to make signs. Plan a get-together before the sale to make signs. This is a great way to engage kids' creativity!

Ask each participant to provide you with a list of their most attractive items so you can include in your ad the items with the most draw.

Encourage families to include their children in the process. Suggest lemonade or soda stands for the youngsters to manage during the sale. Or sell other goodies, such as candy, cookies, coffee and donuts in the morning, and chips and hot dogs for lunch (easily cooked with a small microwave set up outside with an extension cord).

> **HELPFUL HINTS**
>
> *If someone has just a few of a certain type of item—such as toys or books—and someone else has many, ask participants to consider grouping those articles together for better visibility. Create an e-mail group, and include all those involved in the sale. Encourage participants to use the e-mail group to connect with those who have like items. Have individuals who group items keep track through an inventory list or coded price tags.*

Instant Intentions

For at least an hour during the garage sale, arrange to have another family member or friend cover your sale so you can visit each participating neighbor. Try to connect with everyone so that you develop deeper friendships on which to build after the sale. Keep an ear out for those who love shopping garage sales. You may want to set up a day to go garage sale hunting sometime in the near future.

NEIGHBORHOOD MAPPING

idea Although privacy is a serious matter in our culture today, most people want to know and be known by those who live around them. Here is a simple way to give the gift of community to a neighborhood.

Draw an aerial map of the houses you consider to be in your neighborhood, using squares for each house. Put the correct house number by each square, then put your name and the names of your family members in the square representing your house. Also include your phone number. If there are neighbors you already know, put their information in their designated square. Go to these neighbors first, and ask if you can have their permission to include their information on a map that will only be shared with those who add their names.

Pick a good weekend to make the rounds to your other neighbors. Bake lots of fresh chocolate chip cookies to share. At each house, introduce yourself, offer a plate of cookies, and point to the house you live in (so they understand you're a part of the neighborhood). Tell them you are making a map for the neighborhood; if they will write their information on the map, you'll make sure they get a copy.

> ### HELPFUL HINTS
> *Don't share the map with anyone who doesn't agree to include their names. Don't let neighbors use the map for solicitation purposes, and don't make anyone feel that it's wrong to not share their information. You may find that some neighbors want you to have their phone number, but don't want it distributed.*

Make your map extra special by adding color photos of each family. Either have families submit their own photos to you, or offer to take a picture of them. You could also invite your neighbors to each include a family biography (include how long they have lived in the neighborhood, where they're from, where they work, hobbies, and a little about their kids).

Once you have gathered everyone's information, use your computer to make a clean, easy-to-edit map that you can update as people move in and out of the neighborhood. After the map is complete, go back to your neighbors and deliver the finished product. If your neighborhood has not had a published directory before, you'll be amazed at how something little like a map can help neighbors feel connected.

Instant Intentions

Use your completed map to begin recording specific prayers and praying for your neighbors. This is an important first step in inviting God into their lives. The map project is really just the beginning step to making sure the good news about Jesus is shared with everyone in your neighborhood. As you pray, watch for God to begin to open doors to deeper relationships with neighbors who show an interest in spiritual things.

Continue to use your completed map to introduce yourself to new neighbors who move into the neighborhood. Every time there is a change to the map, you have an opportunity to talk to your neighbors while delivering an updated version. After they get more comfortable with your visits, you can begin to ask neighbors if there is anything specific you can be praying about for them.

NEIGHBORHOOD WATCH

idea Most people share a concern for security and safety, particularly when it comes to their homes. This is a way to meet that need while bringing people together.

Convene a neighborhood watch program. Invite people to your house for a dessert and planning meeting. Use this time to draft your own safety programs; lead a conversation about what your neighborhood could do in the event of a fire or natural disaster. Ask if there are elderly in the neighborhood who might need help. Invite people to share work or alternate phone numbers where they could be reached, and create a phone tree that will help alert everyone when needed.

> ### HELPFUL HINTS
> *A page with helpful lists of needed supplies is found at www.ready.gov. They suggest inviting a police officer to one of your meetings if you'd like. There are also online resources, and you can register your group for others to look up. Also, for information on a formal project, see www. usaonwatch.org.*

Some details you might discuss include: what kinds of things most need to be saved (such as family photos or paperwork), a plan of where to go outside the neighborhood, and whether or not anyone would need transportation in an emergency. You could also offer information on what kinds of supplies people ought to keep on hand (such as bottles of water, canned goods, radio, and a flashlight). In addition to disasters or emergencies, you might also cover what to do in case of a crime. Discuss who to call and what to do or not do.

Assure neighbors that, just as in the case of health, preventative measures are the best plan.

Instant Intentions

Don't wait for a natural disaster to start caring for your neighbors. Be on the lookout for your neighbors' everyday needs, such as helping with a lawn. Offer to lend a hand on something small and spontaneous, thus communicating that you care for them in big and little ways.

PACK UP THE VAN

idea With rising energy costs, transportation is not just an issue for the elderly anymore. College kids, unemployed adults, or people just struggling to make ends meet are all in need of help.

If there are people in your neighborhood who need help getting to malls, to the grocery store, to doctor appointments, getting their kids to school, or even getting to work, think about how you and others in your area could step up to fill that need.

First, enlist the aid of other like-minded volunteers in your neighborhood. Then figure out the logistics of the service. Who will be providing transportation? How often will you provide transportation and to where? What days and times will you offer the services? Will you need to rotate volunteers? Are safety and liability issues adequately covered?

Once you have a plan, let your neighbors know of your idea. Use your homeowners' association newsletter, if you have one, to get the word out. Or, you could drop off fliers to each home.

> **HELPFUL HINTS**
>
> *If you find that the need in your neighborhood is more than you can reasonably handle, call in the aid of your local social services department. Many areas have van services for the elderly and disabled. You might even call a local cab company and see if they would be willing to offer discounts to people in need.*

Then begin your service. Don't be afraid to start small. Maybe you'll begin by offering a ride to the mall once a month or to the grocery store once a week. Be clear that you're not an on-call taxi service. But be just as clear that you want to be a resource to help people with genuine needs, especially if a neighbor has an emergency transportation situation.

Then use the time in the car or van to begin building relationships with your passengers. Ask questions to learn more abut their lives, their families, and their needs. Offer to pray with them, and if appropriate, offer to connect them with people in your church who may be able to supply other kinds of assistance.

You might have repeat "customers," and they will spread the word to other neighbors. As you develop relationships, recipients may start asking questions about why you're doing this. What a perfect opportunity to invite them to visit your church where they can learn more about a relationship with God!

PARENTING SEMINAR

idea Even the best of parents need more wisdom from time to time (or reassurance that they really *are* on the right track!). Show that you care about families by hosting a parenting seminar for your neighborhood.

Invite an outside speaker to give talks on topics relevant to your attendees. Choose one or more of the following: especially gifted parents from your church congregation, a local social worker or family counselor, a Red Cross parenting class instructor, or a child development teacher from a local college. You might also include a panel of parents for an open-question session. Among the topics you can discuss:

- how to set boundaries with teenagers
- the challenges of single parenting
- building character in your children
- maintaining a healthy marriage for the sake of healthy children
- insights into how your child's (or teen's) brain really works
- parenting with love and logic

> **HELPFUL HINTS**
>
> *Don't stop at your seminar. Provide opportunities for both your attendees and you to follow up on what they've learned. Invite participants to attend your church or other related events there, or offer short-term small groups on the subject you've covered.*

Provide a pleasant, warm atmosphere. Include a wide selection of refreshments. Invite a few friends from church to attend the event, and use the opportunity to show your neighborhood what a church family looks like, too.

Instant Intentions

If you feel it would be of interest to your audience, include as a topic how to understand and develop your children's faith.

PEN PALS AND FLOWER POTS

idea If you live in an intergenerational neighborhood, here's a great opportunity for kids to interact with the elderly! Each child will develop a relationship with a senior pen pal by writing a letter, decorating a flower pot and planting a flower, then personally delivering his or her note and flower pot.

First, identify the kids and senior citizens willing to participate in your project. Write a brief flier, and hand it to people you think might be interested. Explain your vision with enthusiasm.

> **HELPFUL HINTS**
> *Adapt your plans to meet the needs of participants. If some of your seniors are housebound, accompany the children to deliver the pots and notes in person, rather than having an event at your home. Be sure to set the appointment when it's convenient for the seniors.*

Second, assign one senior to each child. Give the seniors their assigned child's name, and ask that they write a note about themselves to the child, specifying when the letter needs to be delivered by. Set the date prior to when the children will meet to decorate their pots and write their own notes. You can have the seniors mail their letters individually, or you can collect and deliver them in person.

In turn, have each child write a note to his or her assigned senior. If you're dealing with an age group too young to write notes, have them color pictures that show themselves doing something they enjoy. Help each child address or label his or her note to the pen pal.

Once the notes are written, have the children come to your house (or yard, depending on the weather) to decorate flower pots. Use small terra cotta pots, and have the children paint them or glue on decorative craft items. Then fill each pot with dry potting soil, and press some seeds (such as alyssum or baby's breath) into the surface. Print out instructions that say "Water Me and Watch Me Grow" on small slips of paper, and tape them to a toothpick like a small flag. Stick the toothpick flag into the soil of each pot, and you're ready to go.

Invite everyone to your home so kids can meet the seniors and give them the pots and notes. This may also be a good time to let the kids get to know their pen pals better through games or story time, as time allows.

Instant Intentions

Encourage both kids and seniors to keep the relationships going. You could have monthly or bimonthly gatherings at your home, or you could simply ask participants when you see them whether they've connected with their pen pals recently.

SERVING SINGLE PARENTS

idea Twice as many dishes to wash, twice as many rides to school, twice as many shoes to tie, twice as many hugs to give—but only half the energy, half the time, and half the people. Single parents work, and work hard without always having another adult to talk to or a backup when they need a minute to breathe.

Give the single parents in your neighborhood a helping hand by making some of their everyday tasks a little easier. One way is to provide once-a-month babysitting for single parents. If it's on a weeknight, right after school, or on a Saturday morning, it'll give those parents the opportunity to schedule doctor appointments, run to the grocery store, or just have a little downtime.

Consider also offering a monthly or bimonthly night out for these parents, and if you have kids of your own, let all the kids play together during that time.

> **HELPFUL HINTS**
> *You'll want to establish relationships with the single parents in your neighborhood before they allow you to babysit. Invite them to dinner, help them with yardwork, deliver a plate of cookies, or simply give them your phone number and say you're available if they need help.*

Instant Intentions

Invite the single-parent families you serve to come to church with you. Even if the parents don't accept your invitation, ask if you can take their kids to Sunday school and other church events.

SWAP MEET AND GREET

idea Do you have a few still-perfectly-useful-but-not-to-*you*-anymore items lying around your house? Clothes your kids have outgrown? Invite your neighbors to attend this free, no-money-required swap meet.

You will be organizing the time and place for this event, so choose an upcoming weekend afternoon, and scope out a location suitable for a sizeable neighborhood gathering. You might choose a nearby park, an open parking lot, or even your garage. Check with your local parks department or the owner of the lot to make sure you can hold your event in the location.

To advertise the swap meet, post fliers around the neighborhood. If your neighborhood has a Web site or an e-mail chain, send out a digital notice of the event. In the advertisement, ask your neighbors to bring their gently used, still-working items and clothes to the swap meet to give away or trade with others. State that no money will change hands—this is simply a way to "recycle" items that you no longer use and give to someone who will!

> **HELPFUL HINTS**
>
> *If your choice of location doesn't have tables or raised surfaces, try to bring some portable folding tables to set up for displaying smaller items.*
>
> *Consider organizing your swap meet tables into categories so attendees can easily find what they're looking for. For example, try "Lawn and Garden," "Housewares," and "Tools."*

Have large blankets spread out on your grass and large tables to display items. Also have plenty of empty hangers and places to hang clothing. Rope tied between two trees or ladders works well. As neighbors arrive, assist them in displaying their items.

Consider setting up a "kids only" section, where children can come to swap their toys, games, or books. This is also a great area to keep kids occupied by setting up a refreshment station where they can serve lemonade and cookies (or other simple snacks) to the attendees. Within this section, you could also host an area for families to exchange baby and toddler items or for mothers-to-be to find maternity clothing.

Instant Intentions

While you're looking for some new items to acquire, take the time to stop and chat with your neighbors. Ask them what they're looking for, and offer to help them find it. If the item they need is for a specific project or purpose, you could also offer to help them with the project. Exchange phone numbers or addresses with your new acquaintances, and follow up with them to see how you might be able to help them in the future.

WELCOME TO THE NEIGHBORHOOD

idea Show God's love and kindness to those who are new to your neighborhood.

Create a welcome committee with neighbors who are interested in helping those who are new to the neighborhood. Hold an interest meeting at your home or community clubhouse. Hand deliver the invitations, and explain your intent to invite neighbors to gather around and welcome those who are moving into the neighborhood. It would work best for this meeting to be held on a weekday night or weekend, so that everyone will be able to attend.

Provide light refreshments for the meeting. Have poster board or newsprint taped to a wall and a marker for brainstorming ideas.

Once all the guests have arrived, have them sit where they can all see you and the poster board. Begin by welcoming them and sharing a story about how you felt when you were new to a neighborhood. After a few volunteers have shared their own experiences, begin the brainstorming process.

> **HELPFUL HINTS**
> *This committee could also be responsible to help those who are moving out of the neighborhood. They could help the family pack and clean, then throw them a neighborhood going-away party.*

Now discuss ways you can show new neighbors they are welcome in your neighborhood. What are some things newly moved people need? Write down ideas such as toilet paper, paper towels, cleaning supplies, food, and so on. Also brainstorm non-material needs, such as lawn care, help unpacking, furniture-moving, and tips and directions for the city.

After brainstorming, go back through the list and decide as a group the five most important needs of a new neighbor from each list. Once the group has decided what needs are most important, ask for volunteers to be responsible for meeting those needs. For example, the next time someone moves into your neighborhood, Matt is going to be the one to offer to mow their lawn, Angela will take over a basket of cleaning supplies, and Mary will bring them a meal.

Create a master list with names and phone numbers of the committee members. Discuss how you will let each other know when a new neighbor moves in and what needs will be covered.

Instant Intentions

....

When getting to know your new neighbors, be sure to invite them to your church, or suggest other churches in the area that might better fit their style and preferences.

EATING TOGETHER: FOOD-RELATED OUTREACH IDEAS

"They worshiped together at the Temple each day, met in homes for the Lord's Supper, and shared their meals with great joy and generosity—all the while praising God and enjoying the goodwill of all the people."

ACTS 2:46-47

Everyone has to eat, right?

So why not eat with your neighbors? You'll have fun, get to know them better, and gather some great new recipes in the mix. Best of all, you'll nurture relationships that can turn into friendships. Then from friendships, you can take the next important step of sharing your faith.

Who knew that a meal could make so much happen? So grab that cookbook and those oven mitts, and start cookin'!

BAKERY BARTER BONANZA

idea Who doesn't like gooey brownies or chewy cookies? Invite your neighbors to participate in a swap for baked goods, enjoy each other's favorite recipes, and get better acquainted in the process. Invite any and all the bakers on your block, and make the invitation unique. Use a brownie or giant cookie wrapped attractively in colored cellophane and ribbon, and attach it to the invitation. Include the time and place and a description of how you intend to conduct the exchange.

> **HELPFUL HINTS**
> *Provide coffee and tea to encourage neighbors to linger, sample, and become better acquainted. Discuss the possibility of collecting recipes and providing copies for everyone. Also, have plastic wrap and extra plates on hand for those who need a way to take their goodies home. Using non-disposable plates can help ensure follow-up visits for dish return.*

At the beginning of the event, have each person describe what he or she has brought to barter. Encourage the group members to swap samples if they wish. Once they know what they want to take home, have them begin bartering and trading with each other. For instance, the rate might be a cookie for a cookie, or two pieces of pie for four cookies, or a slice of cake for a scone. Give suggestions before beginning, but let the bakers decide, and have fun!

Continue the bartering until everyone has exchanged goodies. If someone's rhubarb bars or zucchini brownies are still to be traded, let the cooks give one each to participants of their choice, and in exchange choose one item from their stash (similar to a "white elephant" gift swap).

Instant Intentions

Did you connect with a person in a new way at the event? Maybe you bonded over a certain delectable sample of fudge, or you got her recipe for something she brought to the exchange. Within a week to 10 days, invite her over to share a cup of coffee or tea, serve the treat you bonded over, and use the opportunity to get to know her better.

BLAST FROM YOUR PAST POTLUCK

idea Everyone has a history. One thing people often remember is food, and, since everybody eats, it's a great way to get to know one another.

Have a Blast From Your Past Potluck. Invite everyone from your neighborhood, and ask them to bring a dish that reflects or is drawn from his or her personal heritage. For instance, maybe someone grew up on a farm and knows exactly what to do with a chicken. Maybe someone's home was in an urban area with lots of local flavor. Or, maybe someone has a favorite dish from their ethnic background. Maybe someone makes the kind of cookies his or her grandmother always made. Offer these kinds of suggestions in your invitation, and encourage people to be creative.

Have everyone bring their dish along with an explanation of its significance. Use what you learn to find out more about the people who come and to let them know more about you.

Instant Intentions

Your heritage can be a powerful tool. If you had a Christ-centered upbringing, you can show your thankfulness for its goodness. Or, you can demonstrate how God has led you throughout your life. Learning about others' pasts can also help you understand them. Learn what you can, now that you have a starting point. If you find out about difficulties someone has had, pray for that person.

> **HELPFUL HINTS**
>
> One way to spice up this party is to have everyone write down their explanations. Then have a contest to see who can match up stories with the people (you'll need to conceal who brought what). To make it even more challenging, have them omit the name of the dish in their explanation and then try to guess both the dish and the person who brought it. Or, if people don't know each other well enough to guess, collect everyone's explanations and recipes and make a little cookbook out of it. If you have a digital camera, you could take pictures and make a photo album out of it, too.

No matter what, show your appreciation and interest in their lives.

BREAD EXCHANGE

idea What's more irresistible than freshly baked bread? Reach out to your neighbors through a delicious loaf of your best recipe. And invite them to share their favorite bread recipe and a sample as well. Bread exchanges are an especially great way to bring ladies together—although there are certainly some men with excellent skill in this area.

A bread exchange can be held any time of the day, any day of the week, and any month of the year. Choose a day and time that best suits the neighbors you want to invite. If they are moms with small children, keep nap times and feeding schedules in mind. If they are working women, it might be best to host your party in the evening after the dinner hour or on a weekend.

Each person invited will be instructed to bake two loaves of her favorite bread. They can be two from the same recipe or two different ones. She will also need to bring copies of her recipe to exchange with others.

Once you have decided on a time and a date, write up an invitation. It should include the time, date, and location of your party, a brief explanation of the exchange, a date to RSVP by, and your phone number. Attach a mini loaf of freshly baked bread wrapped in foil or plastic wrap to your invitation to tantalize neighbors coming to your party.

Before the party, set out empty trays or plates to display the breads. Have coffee or other beverages available and small plates for serving the breads. Butter or other tasty spreads would also be a nice addition to your table.

When all the guests have arrived, welcome them to your home and thank them for sharing their baking and recipes. Explain that each guest may have two slices of each kind of bread, one to sample and one to take home.

Instant Intentions

Send each guest a thank-you note for coming to your bread exchange. At the bottom of your notes, write out the Scripture, *"Jesus replied, 'I am the bread of life. Whoever comes to me will never be hungry again. Whoever believes in me will never be thirsty'"* (John 6:35).

COMMUNITY MYSTERY DINNER

idea Here's a great way for your neighbors to learn more about each other. This activity is especially well-suited to people living in an apartment or planned-community or development setting.

Finding a location to host your mystery event is easy. A neighborhood clubhouse or large basement is perfect. And these days, hosting a mystery dinner is as easy as going to your local game store or searching the Internet, where you can find numerous themed kits that give you everything you need from plots to clues to menus. Everyone loves a meal, and the intrigue gives the party a focal point and keeps everyone involved.

Whether buying a prepared game or coming up with your own mystery, remember these basic tips for a successful event:

> **HELPFUL HINTS**
> Spice up the atmosphere of the event. If costumes are a possibility, wear them. If you have extra people who want to help out, you and they could dress up appropriately as waiters or servants or the master of the hall. For more help in planning a unique scenario, try the local library. You can find dozens of short mysteries in a Miss Marple Investigates or Hercule Poirot Mysteries collection.

1. Encourage your guests to come in costume, and have simple props available for their use.
2. Invite the correct number of guests.
3. Provide character name tags so your guests can remember who they're portraying.
4. Decorate your meeting area to reflect the mystery's theme. Themed food is also a fun addition.

If you're not able to find or buy party kits, you might consider just hosting a themed dinner. Provide each of the guests with a pamphlet giving the details of a mystery to be solved, or you might break it up into sections to be given out or even read aloud between each course. Give everyone a chance to guess the solution.

Send out an open invitation to all neighbors, or, if you live in an apartment complex, post a sign-up sheet on the community bulletin board. Most purchased mystery kits are for six to eight people, so you might consider doing one on a bimonthly basis so everybody has a chance to participate.

Instant Intentions

This can be a great way to show your neighbors that Christians are about living a Christlike life of joy, not just following a bunch of rules. If it turns out that there is anyone at the party who particularly enjoys mysteries, you might offer to do some reading together. A mystery book club is always fun. There are a lot of great mystery writers out there, and their books can provide an opening for further discussions. Try Dorothy Sayers, Agatha Christie, or Ellis Peters for some great material.

DINNER AROUND THE WORLD

idea You may have heard of a progressive dinner party, where you eat a different course of the meal at different friends' homes. Well, this is the same idea, only with a culinary twist. Each stop will include food from a different country. The appetizer could be Mexican or Indian, the main dish Italian or Chinese, and the dessert from yet another country.

Ask three or four different neighbors if they would like to be a part of an "Around the World Dinner Party." Find out who wants to make which course and what country they would like to represent. You will need each person to make one of the following:

- appetizer
- soup and/or salad
- main dish
- dessert

After you have decided who will be preparing what dish, let everyone involved know where to meet for the appetizer and at what time. Keep in mind the length of time it may take you with each course and travel time between houses, when deciding on your start time. You probably want to allow about three hours for the entire event.

Instant Intentions

Before the evening begins, spend some time in prayer asking God to prepare you for the time you will share with your neighbors. Thank him for this great opportunity to show his love to others. Ask him to guide your conversations and be sensitive to what the Holy Spirit might want to say through you.

DINNER BY DESIGN

idea A themed potluck makes a common idea a lot more fun.

Pick a theme that suits you or the time of year: Italian, Hawaiian, 70s, picnic basket, Christmas in July, or green. You get the idea...the possibilities are endless! Buy or make simple invitations, and deliver them personally. Provide a few suggestions so neighbors will know what you're thinking. For example, if you're going green, you might suggest salad, broccoli soup, spinach pasta in pesto sauce, and key lime pie. Don't forget to tell everyone to wear their favorite green T-shirt! This way, folks will know to dress casually as well as bring something that may or may not be salad.

Instant Intentions

Have invitations for the second potluck ready to hand out as guests leave. Fill in everything but the theme and location. Offer your home, but be open to others who'd like to host. Enlist everyone's suggestions for the theme.

HELPFUL HINTS
Here's a recipe for a delicious broccoli soup:

1½ cups chicken broth
½ cup onion, chopped
2 cups chopped broccoli
½ teaspoon thyme
1 bay leaf
dash garlic salt
2 tablespoons butter
2 tablespoons flour
½ teaspoon salt
1 cup milk

Boil first six ingredients for 10 minutes. Remove bay leaf. Blend in blender or food processor till smooth and set aside. Melt butter. Add flour, salt, and a dash of white pepper. Stir in milk. Cook and stir until mixture boils. Add broccoli and heat through. Serves three.

EAT MEAT CLUB

idea Here's an idea to get the guys together...but all family members are welcome. Everyone has a favorite food. Some people hold to their tastes with more passion than others. Often, guys are pretty dedicated to a good steak.

Start an Eat Meat Club in your neighborhood. Send out an invitation to the guys to join you at your house for a barbecue. To be creative, design the invitations to look like a T-bone steak. Invite people to bring their own favorite meat dish or marinade.

Offer a variety of meats and marinades, and declare the inauguration of the neighborhood's Eat Meat Club. Suggest that you all get together for a monthly barbecue at different houses in the neighborhood, and two or three families can be responsible for supplying the food each time. Make sure to provide a vegetarian alternative, such as veggie burgers.

> **HELPFUL HINTS**
>
> *Here's a recipe for a tasty, easy-to-do marinade:*
>
> *1 cup soy sauce*
> *1 cup sesame oil*
> *1 cup hoisin sauce*
> *¹⁄₄ cup brown sugar*
>
> *Mix the ingredients, and let the meat soak overnight. This recipe is best with beef or pork.*

For fun, offer a series of prizes for funny events, like a hot-dog-eating contest or a trivia quiz about cuts of beef.

Instant Intentions

Before eating, lead a very simple prayer to start the meal. Keep in mind that prayer may not be a part of your guests' practices, so use the opportunity to show them how it's done! You might say something as simple as this: "Lord, thank you for this food. Thank you for these friends. Thank you for this time together. In Jesus' name, amen."

Take pictures of your inaugural gathering. Then make sure to designate someone's house for the next meeting. Before then, hand-deliver pictures to everyone who came, as a fun reminder of the event. Use this little visit as a further opportunity to get to know your neighbors.

FINALS FOOD...AND MORE

idea Studying and snacking seem to go hand in hand. Use exam time as an opportunity to start or deepen relationships with the students in your neighborhood. During exam time, commit to delivering snacks to the students in your neighborhood.

Start by identifying the students in your neighborhood, from junior high school through graduate school. Talk to the parents of students younger than college age to tell them of your intentions and get their permission.

Then collect yummy snacks for your students to munch. Prepackaged items are best, such as small bags of nuts, fruit snacks, and trail mix. Then deliver your treats with a note of explanation and encouragement.

Don't limit your efforts to finals time. Make it a habit to keep in touch with the students in your neighborhood. Use any school activities or other activities as an excuse. Know of a big game or meet coming up? Stop by with a sports drink and an energy bar. Do you know of a student who recently preformed in a school play or concert? If you make it to the event, write a "bravo" note on a blank CD-R to tell the student that one day, he or she might just have a CD of his or her own.

Once you've established a relationship with students and their parents during the school year, you can continue to connect with them all year—not just during finals time.

Instant Intentions

If you feel the time and relationship is right, don't be afraid to tuck a faith-based note of encouragement in with the snacks. Consider including a favorite Bible verse and a note saying you'll be praying for the recipient. (Then don't forget to pray!)

NEIGHBORHOOD COOKING CLASS

idea Some people know the secret to getting barbecue grilling right every time. Wouldn't you love to know how? Or what about other cooking tips like how to make crème brûlée or homemade bread?

Ask around the neighborhood, and find those who would be interested in sharing their techniques in the kitchen or back yard. Once you've found two or three culinary artists, decide on a time, date, and location to hold a cooking class for everyone in the neighborhood. This would be a great experience for young married couples, families, or older teenagers about to leave home for the first time.

You can create your own invitations or use the sample on the following page.

Instant Intentions

Depending on how many cooks you find, hold one or more classes. If you find several interested cooks, hold a class once a month. You might begin to strategically include certain genres of food or types of dishes in your classes. For instance, one month you might explore French cooking and Asian the next. For more advanced training, you and a few neighbors might want to experience more professional cooking classes together. Use this opportunity to get to know each other better and learn from one another.

> **HELPFUL HINTS**
>
> *Here are some helpful kitchen tips you can use to amaze your neighbors.*
>
> *Add a tablespoon of sugar and a splash of lemon juice to the water you boil corn in to make corn on the cob extra tasty.*
>
> *To avoid the dangerous possibility of undercooked chicken when grilling, boil it first in a pot of water on the stove.*
>
> *Soften an onion in the microwave by first chopping it and then microwaving it for about a minute.*

—Cooking Class—

Want to brush up on your culinary skills?

You are invited to a neighborhood cooking class.
Some of your talented neighbors are willing
to share their skills and their creations.

WHEN:

WHERE:

Please call and let me know you're coming!

MY NAME:

PHONE:

PROGRESSIVE DINNER PARTY

idea Have a party! Invite everyone on your block to participate in a progressive dinner party. It's a great way to get to know everyone better and have a lot of fantastic food and fun.

If you plan the dinner during nice weather, driveways can be the stopping place as the group progresses around the block. A grill is a great way to keep food warm. Also, have diners bring their own lawn or camp chair and just take it along from house to house. Also, determine if dinnerware will be provided at each home or if neighbors need to bring the right supplies with them.

Send out invitations and ask everyone to choose what they'd like to serve. If someone doesn't cook but wants to participate, encourage them to provide a beverage station—a place to stop along the way to refill drinks. Organize the courses in a logical order, and plan the progression. Once you have a head count, pass that information on to all participating hosts. A sample invitation is provided to give an idea for your own invitation. Start by meeting at your own home for the first course at the designated time. Then, once you're ready,

> **HELPFUL HINTS**
>
> ### Progressive Dinner Party Appetizer
>
> *Potato wedges are always a hit and a lot easier than the potato skins restaurants serve. Cut potatoes into wedges—about eight per potato. Toss in a bowl with olive oil and sprinkle with your favorite seasoning salt. Place in foil or a grill basket (or directly on rack if perpendicular to the grate) and cook over medium heat for about 20 minutes or until golden brown. (These can also be cooked in the oven at 450 degrees in a single layer on a cookie sheet.) Serve with sour cream, ketchup, ranch dressing or any other favorite sauce.*

move together to the next house. Encourage cooks to prepare items that can easily be kept warm or served cold so that they won't have to miss the festivities.

Instant Intentions

Within a week or two after your block party, invite one of the families or a few of the singles you became acquainted with over for dinner or dessert and a game night. See page 58 or 94 for ideas.

Dear Neighbor,

How about a progressive dinner block party? We'd love to have you join us as we move around the neighborhood, sharing a different course at each home. You can prepare anything from an appetizer to a dessert. Choose a course you'd like to host and let us know. Or, if cooking's not your thing, how about providing a beverage station? We'll bring our own chairs, meet in each host's driveway, and share food and fun before advancing to the next course. Dinnerware, cups, and utensils will be provided along the way. Just can't manage to host this time? Let us know and join us in the progression anyway. We'd love to have you there! The party will be on_____starting at _____p.m. in our driveway. We'll start the meal off with some beverages and yummy appetizers. Thanks!

Your name
Your phone number, e-mail address, and street address

RECIPE RALLY

idea Undoubtedly, there are a lot of great cooks in your neighborhood who would love to share their recipes. It's always fun to get new recipes and cooking ideas from others. Have a neighborhood recipe rally with a potluck of samples, and then create a neighborhood cookbook.

Write up a simple invitation letting your neighbors know you'd like to compile a neighborhood cookbook. Ask them to bring recipes from these categories: appetizers, main dishes, side dishes, and desserts. They can bring more, but they need to offer at least one from each category. Ask everyone to also make one of their recipes to bring to a potluck for others to sample.

Choose a Saturday when everyone can attend, including children. Be sure to include an RSVP date so you will know how many guests will be attending and how many recipes will be coming in. That way, if you don't have a decent amount of recipes, you can supplement

> **HELPFUL HINTS**
> *If you live in a neighborhood with lots of young children, include a section in the cookbook for kids' non-food recipes, such as modeling dough, bubbles, and sidewalk chalk. These kinds of recipes can easily be found on the Internet.*

with more of your own. Also, be sure to ask guests for a $2 donation to cover your costs in printing the cookbooks.

On the day of the party, set out plates, silverware, and drinks. Have places for people to sit and eat and plenty of chairs around the house or lawn if it's a nice day. After everyone has arrived, give a welcome and thank them for being willing to share their recipes. Allow your guests to eat the food that everyone has brought and mingle with other neighbors.

After everyone has finished eating, collect all the recipes. Be sure your guests have their names written on their recipes so you can give credit to them in the cookbook. Explain that you will deliver the finished cookbooks after you have put them together. Allow yourself about two weeks to make the cookbooks.

You can either take all the recipes to a print shop and have the books made for you, or you can retype them all on your computer and bind them with a plastic spring binder (from a print or craft shop) for a less expensive alternative. Be sure you keep the recipes within their specific category. Make a cover for the cookbook using card stock, and title it with the name of your neighborhood and the year.

Instant Intentions

Consider sprinkling Scripture verses throughout the book. Choose an easy-to-understand version of the Bible, such as the New Living Translation (NLT).

SALSA SMACKDOWN

idea What's your favorite salsa? Is it a lime-corn salsa, a spicy habanero salsa, or a sweet and tangy mango salsa? Mouth watering yet? Get creative with your cooking, and enter your best-concocted salsa recipe into a contest with your neighbors.

Two weeks before your party, send out invitations. Let your neighbors know they are to bring their best salsa recipe and some for everyone to sample. Decide on whether or not you want to serve a full meal or just appetizers to go with the chips and salsa. Then be sure to let your guests know what to expect.

On the day of your party, set out enough bowls for all of the competing salsas. Place a score sheet and a pen by each bowl of salsa. Have plenty of tortilla chips for tasting the salsas and plenty of drinks for cleansing palates.

> **HELPFUL HINTS**
> *Make copies of the score sheet below for each salsa, and fill in the salsa's name on each score sheet before the contest.*

After everyone has tasted the salsas, tally the votes and award something to the winner of the highest score. You might also give a token of appreciation to every participant; a nice kitchen utensil, cookbook, a bag of jalapeños or red peppers, or a jar of gourmet salsa would all work well.

— Salsa Smackdown —
SCORE SHEET
(Give each salsa a score from 1 to 5 for each category, 1 being the best.)

SALSA NAME:

APPEARANCE:

FLAVOR:

ORIGINALITY:

You cannot vote for your own salsa!

Instant Intentions

If you plan to serve a meal at the party, have your guests gather before you eat to say a blessing over the meal. Lead them in a simple prayer, thanking God for the opportunity to be together and for the food you are about to eat. End the prayer on a light note, saying, "…and give us the courage to try all this salsa!"

SHARE A CSA SHARE

idea Everyone needs groceries. If you live close to an agricultural area, buying a CSA (Community Supported Agriculture) share is a fun and practical way to meet needs—and form friendships.

CSA farms are more and more common these days. All you need to do is lay down a payment at the beginning of summer, and the fresh fruits and vegetables roll in all season long. CSA shares can be too big for one family, though, so it's a great idea to find someone else who is interested, then split both the cost and the spoils. Besides enjoying the material benefits, you'll get the chance to meet your neighbors and the local farmers.

Even if you don't share the food, joining a CSA with other households can be rewarding. Some CSA farms even have special festivals or potlucks to celebrate the end of the season, or the corn or pumpkin harvests. Consider experiencing these events with your neighbors. It's fun, it's a great way to feel more connected to the food you eat and the place you live, and it's a great community builder for a neighborhood.

Instant Intentions

Sharing a CSA share can be a great springboard to further relationships. Beyond meeting to share your spoils, why not use it as a chance to have a dinner with food from your produce? When the winter comes, try to keep up the relationship. If you get in the habit of meeting during the summer, you'll be more likely to continue throughout the year. Also, be sure to take advantage of the opportunity to thank God for his bounty.

> **HELPFUL HINTS**
>
> If you're not sure where to find a CSA farm in your area, try your local farmers market. If there aren't any CSAs in your area, why not make a plan to visit the farmers market as a neighborhood and go in together on bushels of produce? You can get your food cheaper in bulk and then divide it.
>
> If you're looking for unique ways to serve, you might consider sponsoring a needy family by purchasing or subsidizing a share for them.

SOUP SWAP

idea There's nothing better than a steaming cup of soup on a cold winter's day. OK maybe there is. How about sharing it with a friend? Better yet, how about your friend sharing his or her soup with you? How about a bunch of friends and neighbors sharing their favorite soup recipes with each other and enjoying their company over several different samples of soup?

A soup swap can be done any time of the year but may hold more appeal in the colder months. It can be done as a simple lunch or an elaborate full-course dinner. Decide on the time of day, and create a guest list based on which neighbors you know will be available at the hour you plan to hold your party.

> **HELPFUL HINTS**
> *For smaller groups of only three or four guests, the soup swap game may not be as fun. In this case, have the group stand in a circle with their soup, and ask them to pass their soup one person to the left.*

Write up an invitation explaining that each guest will need to bring a favorite soup recipe and a jar of at least four servings—or 4 to 5 cups—of that soup. Be sure to include on the invitation your address, phone number, and an RSVP date.

On the day of the party, set out drinks, bowls, spoons, napkins, and bread or crackers for soup dipping. As guests arrive, give each person a number from one to the highest number of guests who attend. Have guests place their jars of soup on a table or countertop where everyone can see them. Also, have recipes with the names of the soup clearly displayed near each soup container.

Ask guests to sit in a circle to play Soup Swap, which is similar to a white elephant gift exchange. Explain that the person who has number one will go first and can select a soup of choice. After selecting a soup, the person sits down with it. Then the person with number two takes a turn picking a soup; this person can either choose a new soup or can take the first soup that was chosen. If Number Two chooses a new soup, then it is Number Three's turn. If Number Two takes the soup of

Number One, Number One has to pick a new soup. Number Three can pick either Number One or Two's soup or pick a new soup. The game continues this way until the last person's turn. The person with the last number can pick any soup he or she wants from the group. If the person chooses a soup other than the last soup remaining, the person he or she took the soup from has to take the last unclaimed jar of soup.

Instant Intentions

Make a bunch of mini loaves of bread for each guest to take home with their soup. Attach a small card letting your neighbors know you are glad to be their neighbor, and write out an encouraging Scripture such as, *"I pray that God, the source of hope, will fill you completely with joy and peace because you trust in him. Then you will overflow with confident hope through the power of the Holy Spirit"* (Romans 15:13).

SUPER SUPPER CLUB

idea Use this meal-making time to ease everyone's week, while growing friendships with your neighbors.

Plan several simple, freezable suppers, and then invite several neighbors to join you in preparing enough meals for everyone's families to eat during the week. Choose meals appropriate for you and your neighbors. You could plan home-style casseroles like spaghetti pie, vegetable sides like orange-glazed carrots, or gourmet dishes like veal cutlets *cordon bleu*.

There are many options for covering the cost. Create the grocery list with amounts needed for each item. Don't forget the pans for everyone to use to take their meals home—unless you've asked them to bring certain ones. Choose what's best for you and your neighbors.

Other ideas:
- Do the shopping and save the receipt for dividing later.
- Ask each guest to bring certain ingredients.
- Ask each guest to bring their own favorite recipe and the ingredients for everyone.
- Provide the ingredients as a gift.

When everyone arrives, spend two hours cooking and getting to know each other. Discuss recipes, seasonings, and families.

Instant Intentions

Have some fun recipe books and snacks at a table away from the food prep area. Sit down together for 15 minutes. Snack and plan your next super supper get-together.

ULTIMATE TASTING PARTY

idea Here's a chance for neighbors to get to know each other through a unique food experience.

Host an ultimate tasting party: cheese for some, bread for others, chocolate for another. Have all three food elements and more if you like. This party is great for medium-sized groups; invite singles, families, and couples in your neighborhood.

The key to this activity is to have each person or household bring something different. Try to have at least three different kinds of each food category; the more diversity, the better. A long table or several small tables are essential, so you can lay everything out. Nobody needs to cook; all you need is plates and utensils. Be sure to provide a variety of beverages, such as lemonade, iced tea, soft drinks, and coffee.

As a fun addition to the party, make a list of all the different types and categories of food, so people can rank the items as they try them. That way, everyone will go home with an idea of what they enjoy the most.

Instant Intentions

A great way to follow up on this party is to pay attention to your neighbors' favorites. Then, when they're not expecting it, surprise each person or household with an individualized gift. They'll know you were paying attention, and they'll appreciate your thoughtfulness.

> **HELPFUL HINTS**
> These days, finding good cheese is relatively easy, thanks to specialty sections at the supermarket; however, you may need to try your local kitchen shop for exotic chocolates. Hunt your bakeries for interesting breads, aiming for varieties of texture, not just taste. Once you have the ranking results of the tasting, you can applaud the most popular varieties of the evening. Or, you might have a blind taste test to see if people can tell the difference between brands and types of cheese, bread, and chocolate.

SPORTS AND OUTDOOR FUN

*"And let us run with endurance the race
that God has set before us. We do this by keeping
our eyes on Jesus, the champion who initiates
and perfects our faith."*

HEBREWS 12:1B-2A

Every neighborhood has them—sports fans who proudly display banners, caps, jackets, and signs honoring their favorite teams. Capitalize on the interest and enthusiasm your neighbors show for sports by building relationships that start with sports.

Watch games together. Discuss standings. Second-guess coaching strategies. From there, you can even move to actually engaging in sporting contests together.

The ideas in this chapter can help anyone—from star athletes to those who were chosen last in dodge ball—use sports to score points and develop friendships with their neighbors. After that, the goal is to introduce your new teammates to Jesus, the greatest star of all time.

COMPUTER GAME TOURNAMENT

idea Many people—young and old alike—are passionate about computer games. Why not bring a bunch of computers to your home and have a tournament? The entry fee can be a couple of cans of food for the local food bank, and you can offer a plaque or trophy for the winner.

If bringing computers to your home isn't feasible, have contestants play at home, with everyone starting and ending at the same time. For fun, you may want to appoint monitors with cell phones to make sure everyone starts and stops simultaneously. Then have everyone gather at your house for food, fun, and awards.

> **HELPFUL HINTS**
> *Contact a local video game vendor for ideas about which games would be best for your tournaments. Also, you might need to rent games for players who don't own specific games.*

Be sure to choose games that are not multilevel and that can be completed in a reasonable period of time. Ask the teenagers and young adults of your neighborhood for suggestions. Some games can be judged on best time, others on most points. For games that are won according to most points, stipulate a reasonable period of time to play.

Depending on the number of contestants, you may need to have age categories. If interest is high, consider having an all-day tournament with several games.

Try to have an award for every contestant. For those players who didn't win an actual game, have a good sport award, a fast fingers award, and runner-up awards. Awards can be certificates, plaques, gift certificates, or even home-baked goods. The idea is building community, not competition.

Instant Intentions

This tournament may offer a great opportunity for you to share a bit about your faith. If someone suggests a game that you find objectionable, be ready to explain the reasons behind your decisions in a non-threatening and non-judgmental way.

EXERCISE BUDDIES

idea Here's a great way to get to know a neighbor and get some exercise in the process!

Ask around to see if any of your neighbors would like to join you as a workout partner: jogging, bicycling, swimming, simple free weights at home, or going to a local gym together. Arrange to exercise together at least two or three times a week. Knowing that someone else is counting on you will help both of you stay motivated and faithful to the workout!

As you exercise together, ask your neighbor about his or her family, job, and hobbies. As you build muscle, you'll also be building a relationship that will naturally deepen with time. Discussing the goals you have for your exercise program can be a great springboard for discussing other goals you hope to reach in life. That in turn may someday lead to a discussion of the ultimate goal: heaven!

So get out there—you have nothing to lose but a little weight. And you just might gain a few good friends.

> **HELPFUL HINTS**
>
> *Did you know this? Adults 18 and older need 30 minutes of physical activity five or more days a week to stay healthy. Children and teens need 60 minutes of activity a day for optimal health.*
>
> *(Source: "Physical Activity Fact Sheet," U.S. Dept. of Health and Human Services, www.fitness.gov.)*

Instant Intentions

As you learn more about your neighbor and he or she shares about difficult times or stresses, ask if you may pray for him or her during those times.

FLAG FOOTBALL

idea A friendly neighborhood game usually draws a younger crowd and is a favorite with the children. One day of fun could grow into a weekly neighborhood competition.

A few weeks before the big game, send out invitations or post announcements for the neighborhood game. Make sure you include the time (such as Saturday morning), place (a nearby park or large yard), contact number, and a request for RSVP. You might want to also include a small disclaimer like: "Everyone plays for fun and at their own risk." Follow up about a week before the game with a reminder call to your neighbors.

Recruit a few close friends or neighbors to arrive early with you. Set up cones to mark off the field. You can purchase flags that clip around players' waists for the game at a sporting goods store. For a cheaper option, just play Two-Below. In this version, the offensive player with the ball is down if he or she is touched below the waist with both of a defensive player's hands.

Warm up by playing catch with your family or friend so your neighbors see it's time to join in. Choose teams by having the two youngest people on the field be captains. You can play with as few as six people. If you have more than 20, you probably should split the group so you have two separate games going simultaneously.

When you have enough players to start the game, go over the basic guidelines and field boundaries. Stress that the goal of the game is to have fun rather than relive the glory days of high school. Make certain that everyone is careful and the game remains safe, especially for the sake of the smaller children.

> **HELPFUL HINTS**
>
> *To keep the fun going and to make a lasting connection, invite the football teams over to your home for a chili lunch. Share glory stories about the game, and invite neighbors who weren't interested in playing the game.*
>
> *This outreach works great in all sorts of weather. Rain or snow makes the game a little more dangerous, but it always makes it more interesting.*

People are usually very open to prayer when they are about to put themselves at risk for twisted ankles or torn muscles. Start your game with prayer asking God for safety, and add levity to the prayer by asking God to help the older players remember they aren't in high school anymore.

And remember, one week of football fun can easily turn into a weekly tournament. After the event, check with the players to see if there is interest in keeping the games going. If so, consider recruiting an assistant or two to help you organize the game. Choose a person with whom you've wanted to connect. Working together will give you a chance to go a little deeper with your assistant.

FLOWER BULB AND SEED SWAP

idea Use your thinned-out plants and harvested seeds to reach out to neighbors and share the beauty of flowers. If you have dividable plants, like hens and chicks, daffodils, irises, or shasta daisies, you have all you need to offer your neighbors the benefit of your green thumb.

First, determine what you have in your garden that can be shared with your neighbors. If you aren't certain how or when to thin or collect clippings or seeds, use online or library resources to find the best times and ways to divide or collect from your particular plants.

> **HELPFUL HINTS**
> When you make your list, print it out on an index card or half-page card stock, using color ink and including clip art or pictures of your favorite flowers. You may choose to have it laminated.

Print out a list of the available plants and seeds you'd like to share. Include your name and contact information and when which items will be available. Distribute this information to neighbors—both those with and without gardens. Explain what you'd like to do, and ask if they have plants they would like to share with you or other neighbors. Offer to help them make or distribute their list if they don't think they'll have the time.

If you have seeds available at the time of your list distribution, consider sealing and labeling them in envelopes and taking them to each door. Open the conversation by offering an envelope of seeds, and then explain your plan to share among the neighborhood gardeners.

Instant Intentions

If you don't have the plants to share but would like to use this idea to connect with neighbors, go to the gardeners in your neighborhood who obviously have a green thumb, and let them know you'd like to start a garden. Ask them for any advice about gardening in your area, and ask if they're willing to share any clippings or thinned plants. As time passes and your new garden produces, take a few blossoms to those who helped you.

NEIGHBORHOOD BASEBALL

idea Rally the neighborhood for a fantastic afternoon or summer evening of old-fashioned recreation. Playing baseball together builds camaraderie and companionship.

Often, a last-minute pick-up game works great to pull together people lounging on an idle afternoon. Make phone calls, or knock on doors one to three hours before meeting to give the heads-up that a game is being organized. Choose a large yard or nearby park for your location. Make sure you have any needed equipment. If you lack certain items, ask neighbors to bring them along when you invite them. If they know you're counting on their ball or bat, they'll be more likely to show.

Encourage those who don't play to come along for the snacks and to cheer along the players. Invite them to bring any food items they wish to share, and let them know you'll have some of your favorite brownies or chips and dip there with drinks for them to enjoy as they watch. Remind them to bring their chairs, if needed.

> **HELPFUL HINTS**
> *The Civil War played a crucial role in spreading the diversionary game of baseball. Union soldiers played it for recreation, as other Union troops and Confederate prisoners watched. Thus, when these spectators returned home from the war, baseball spread to many parts of the country. Soon after, everyone from urban dwellers to country farmers made baseball part of their socializing and leisure.*

Instant Intentions

Don't let the gathering break up without asking when everyone wants to meet for another game. Survey everyone to determine the details. Decide a place and time, and discuss who will bring refreshments. Also, take note of which neighbors didn't attend, and be sure to let them know about the next game.

NEIGHBORHOOD CAMP OUT

idea Nothing says summer and brings a sense of togetherness like a warm evening under the stars. Gather the neighborhood children and their parents for a camp out, complete with hot dogs and s'mores, sleeping bags, and tents.

Choose a nearby park, open space, or large yard for your camp out. When deciding on your location, make sure you find out if it will be a place you can use a barbecue grill or camp stove. If not, decide on an alternative food, such as cold sandwiches and chips.

> **HELPFUL HINTS**
>
> *Orion is one of the easiest constellations to locate. It is distinguished by the row of three bright stars, which make up Orion's belt. The bright star above the belt and to the left is called Betelgeuse or Alpha Orionis, Orion's left "shoulder."*

Invite neighbors and inform them of the time and location of the campout. Ask them to bring their camping gear and any extras they would be willing to lend to those who don't have anything.

Bring roasting skewers or wire hangers; hot dogs and all the fixings; and plenty of marshmallows, graham crackers, and chocolate for s'mores. Also have drinks, lanterns and flashlights, and wet wipes for sticky fingers and faces.

Find a neighbor who plays guitar and can lead everyone in some traditional campfire songs. Before dark, play a few family-friendly games such as a three-legged race, freeze tag, or kickball. As the stars appear, lie on your backs and see how many constellations people can name.

Instant Intentions

When stargazing, you might say something about how great God is to create such a huge, beautiful universe. Mention how amazing you think it is that he holds the whole world in the palm of his hands. Also, if you or someone else does play guitar, throw a few praise and worship songs into the mix of campfire songs.

NEIGHBORHOOD SPLASH DAY

idea On a hot summer day, get to know your neighbors better by organizing a neighborhood splash day, a fun and wet time for the whole family!

Find a central location with lots of grass. A large yard or park would work best. Be sure there is a water source close by, then go crazy with the options for getting wet. Have lots of the following available for everyone to use:

- water guns
- water balloons
- sponges
- plastic wading pools
- sprinklers and hoses

Offer a variety of get-wet games, such as water balloon dodge ball, a slippery slide made from a tarp and garden hose, and squirt gun tag.

Post signs a week or so in advance at the entrances to your neighborhood briefly describing the event. Your sign could look something like this:

> **HELPFUL HINTS**
> *Did you know some experts believe that time spent in the sun every day can make you healthier and happier? Nevertheless, take the right precautions. Have extra sunscreen, dry towels, and drinking water available for those who don't have their own.*

It's hot, and it's time to get wet!
Join us for a Neighborhood Splash Day
Fun for the Whole Family
Free Carwash, too!
Date: XX
Time: XX

Instant Intentions

Begin your day with the intention of making a new friend and inviting him or her (and family) over for a barbecue in the evening after the splash day event. Pray and ask God to show you who it is he wants you to invite. Keep your eyes and ears open—and be bold!

NEIGHBORHOOD VEGETABLE GARDEN CO-OP

idea Why not use all that extra zucchini as a way to get to know your neighbors better? Organize a gardening co-op among your neighbors, and help everyone connect while sharing their homegrown produce.

Hold a planning meeting in the spring before planting season begins, where everyone can get acquainted and choose which vegetables they want to grow. Determine the guidelines. For instance, will you swap one for one, or pound for pound? Will you allow IOUs or credit vouchers? How will you handle extra produce?

Then determine who will grow what. If someone already produces great tomatoes but never has luck with corn, have him or her contribute containers of tomatoes. Have each person focus on just a few vegetables (although fruit is great, too!). Choose a nice variety of produce to be disbursed and grown among the gardeners.

As the crops start ripening, set one day per week as the swap day. For example, if it's to be Saturdays at 9 a.m., have everyone meet in a designated driveway to display their harvest.

> **HELPFUL HINTS**
> *Organic and natural farming is becoming more and more popular. Determine within your group if everyone wants to garden without chemicals or pesticides. If so, you can all research what natural alternatives are available, then decide on a course of action. A group outing to your local garden center might be a fun and informative field trip!*

Instant Intentions

Use some of the produce from your co-op to make a tasty dish or canned food item that you can share with your newly acquainted neighbors. For example, if you offer cucumbers for pickles or make a delicious zucchini lasagna, take some to one of your co-op partners to enjoy. Or better yet, invite some neighbors over to enjoy the whole lasagna dinner with you!

SLEDDING SOCIAL

idea Tired of the blast of winter? Then hit the slopes and have your own blast! Follow up with a hot chocolate party to thaw those frozen toes.

After an adequate snowfall, find a great local hill and call all snow lovers to join you. Bring extra sleds or saucers, inner tubes, or even flat pieces of cardboard.

Once you're all sledded out and too cold for even one more run, invite everyone to meet at your home for hot drinks and snacks. Remember, too, warm cookies are a welcomed treat after snow fun. You can use oven-ready cookie dough to have fresh-baked cookies in minutes.

Spend some time sharing; for instance, people can describe their favorite or scariest sledding story. Take a vote on who flew the fastest and longest that day and which type of sled was best. You might even want to explore who has the most creative snow gear, such as hat or interesting layers, as people often improvise in very imaginative ways to stay warm.

Instant Intentions

Once the weather breaks, reunite your sledding buddies by organizing a bike ride. This time, end with a gathering to share cold drinks with chips and salsa, or even bike to your nearest ice-cream shop and indulge in some frozen confectionery together.

> **HELPFUL HINTS**
> It's fun to load as many people as you can onto a long sled or link up several inner tubes before you fly down the slope. But you'll be hard-pressed to beat a record set in 1989 in Wisconsin. One hundred and eighty-seven people piled onto a 120-foot toboggan. The hill they descended was 220 feet long. One must wonder if the last passengers even knew they'd started by the time they ended on such a short hill.

SHOOTING IN THE BREEZE

idea Anyone up for a game of hoops? Or volleyball? Or even inner tube water polo? Unite your neighbors by inviting them to form a recreational sports league team.

Start by researching different venues that accept new teams, like your local city recreational leagues. Find out league schedules and fees, and then invite people to join you. If your neighborhood has a Web site or an e-mail chain, send out a notice. Or, to inspire even more participation, go door to door on a Saturday afternoon and invite your neighbors to play. Let them know it will be a great chance to socialize with neighbors as well as a fun way to get a little of that always-needed exercise.

Once you have gathered a complete team, set up a few meetings or short practices so that all of the players can get to know each other and become comfortable in a team sense before the actual league games start. This is also a great time to discuss each member's skill set and decide who would like to play in each position. Take down your neighbors' contact information, and set up a communication tree so that, if necessary, you can notify your teammates of any changes or updates to your season's schedule.

> ### HELPFUL HINTS
> Consider buying T-shirts or uniforms for team members to increase the sense of team unity. Ask your neighbors if they (or anyone they know) would be willing to become a business sponsor of your team. The sponsors can help pay for the shirts in exchange for printing their logo on the clothing. In addition, try to arrange carpools with your neighbors to and from the sporting events.

Instant Intentions

Don't let the fun stop with the day's final score. After the game each week, invite your teammates to join you for refreshments at a local eatery or coffee shop. These spirited, play-by-play rehashes can turn into much more than just a snack break—they can become great times to connect beyond game play into real-life issues.

STREET HOCKEY

idea Nothing brings out the children in your neighborhood like a game of hockey in the middle of the street.

The most important consideration in street hockey is to make sure everyone is safe from traffic. Choose a quiet street or cul-de-sac, and set up safety cones on both sides of your playing area. Consider asking everyone to play with tennis shoes instead of in-line skates. You can provide hockey sticks and a puck (look for them at used sporting-goods stores) or brooms and a tennis ball.

A few weeks before the big game, send out invitations or post announcements for the neighborhood game. Make sure you include the time (Saturday mornings always work well), place, contact number, and a request for RSVP. You might want to also include a small disclaimer like: "Everyone plays for fun and at their own risk." Follow up a week before the game with a reminder call or visit.

> **HELPFUL HINTS**
> To set the tone of a friendly neighborhood game, purchase an inexpensive, plastic street hockey set with extra plastic sticks. The equipment shows that you're playing hockey (instead of broom ball) and that you're in it for fun—not blood.

Set up two goals with cones or nets. Then go over the basic rules, such as what constitutes a goal, where the boundaries are, and so on. Stress that the goal of the game is to have fun rather than body-check your opponent to the ground. Make certain that everyone takes care to avoid running over the smaller children. If you have an especially competitive group of neighbors, you might want to recruit a referee or have two separate games for the adults and children.

Instant Intentions

When it comes to reaching your neighborhood, winning is nothing; the way you play the game is everything. While you play, laugh a lot and work to include everyone. When you have a chance, take a dive for the children so they can feel the thrill of scoring a goal. Remember that the goal of this game is to build relationships and show the love of Christ.

TANDEM DOG WALKING

idea Here's a great way for dog owners to get to know their canine-loving neighbors. And it doesn't take any extra time—you need to walk your own dog anyway!

Keep an eye out for nearby neighbors who also have dogs, and ask if you and your dog can join them on their walk. If your dogs get along well, try to make it a daily habit. When people walk together every day, they can't help but talk together and eventually get to know each other.

If you pass other dog walkers on your trips, invite them to join you. Soon you may have a whole dog-walking club!

Your conversations will likely be about your dogs at first—how long you've had your pets, which vets you use, training issues, and funny pet stories. But as you feel more comfortable together, the relationship will grow deeper, opening up opportunities for spending time together away from your dogs!

Instant Intentions

After you've exhausted the conversation about each other's dogs, jobs, and families, ask your new friends about things like where and how they grew up, and how they would ideally spend their time if money was not an object. Building relationships is what it's all about! Soon you'll naturally delve into deeper waters, including your faith.

INDOOR FUN
AND FRIENDSHIP

"If you love your neighbor, you will fulfill the requirements of God's law. For the commandments say, 'You must not commit adultery. You must not murder. You must not steal. You must not covet.' These—and other such commandments—are summed up in this one commandment: 'Love your neighbor as yourself.'"

ROMANS 13:8B-9

Your home is your haven from the world, but it can also be used to reach the world. Open your doors to your neighbors, and invite those relationships in!

While the days of neighbors sitting on the front stoop together seem to be dwindling, you can still create a real feeling of friendliness and hospitality in your neighborhood with a few simple steps.

Use the fun ideas in this chapter to get to know your neighbors in a non-threatening, natural way. Play games together. Laugh together. Share stories. As friendships deepen, you'll be able to share with your neighbors the most important friendship of all—friendship with Jesus.

ALL ABOUT THE ACADEMY AWARDS

idea Invite your neighbors over to help celebrate the biggest night for movies in Hollywood—the televised Oscar ceremony.

Start by delivering invitations that cleverly play off the theme; try working one or more movie titles into your verbiage, or use movie-related imagery. For added flair, include small movie trinkets for each person, such as "admit one" tickets.

To set the stage in your home, play a compilation of movie themes as guests arrive. Soundtracks are available for purchase in most music stores, or you could create your own mix from your personal music files. Decorate with glitzy gold, black, and white accessories, or display an arrangement of old movie posters or memorabilia. Make sure you have plenty of comfortable seating.

> **HELPFUL HINTS**
> *The televised ceremony can run late. In order for your neighbors with young children to be able to come, you may want to look into hiring a group babysitter to come to your home for the evening.*

For a more casual party, serve appetizers such as popcorn balls, nachos, and boxes of movie candy. For a touch of elegance, serve smoked salmon rolls, filled puff-pastry triangles, and cheesecake. For added fun, prepare your own ballots listing the major category nominees, and have guests mark who they think will win each award before the show starts. Switch ballots with a neighbor, and keep track of which answers your neighbor guessed correctly as they announce the winners during the ceremony.

Instant Intentions

Before the party, study up on the films, actors, producers, and directors that have been nominated for awards. Take special note of any films that portray good values and any involving people that seem to have led interesting or thought-provoking lives. At the party, if the opportunity comes up, you can mention trivia tidbits. For example, you could say, "I've read about this director—he volunteers his time serving food at homeless shelters. Has anyone here ever done that before?"

BLOCK BOOK CLUB

idea A book club is a great way to spend time discussing important issues and exploring ideas in ways ordinary conversation doesn't allow.

Organize a book club with people on your block. Use local library or online resources to help you determine book lists and develop a format.

Contact your neighbors to announce the start-up of your book club. Lay out your ideas for structure and content, and ask for additional input. Hold an initial get-together to hammer out the details. Consider a rotating meeting place, from home to home, with the host providing light snacks or drinks.

Plan to meet about once a month, exploring a new book each meeting. If your group prefers not to follow a guided discussion, use a loose structure that allows conversation to go wherever the group takes it. You might develop a few basic launching questions to use each time; for instance, "What stood out most to you from the book?"

> **HELPFUL HINTS**
> *Oftentimes, cities will have established book clubs open to visitors or new members. Check with your local library for such clubs, and consider attending at least one before launching your own. You may gain valuable insight into what works well—and what doesn't.*

Instant Intentions

Choose books that give good examples of the human condition. Remember, books don't have to be categorized as "Christian" books to speak truth about pain and suffering or the many other situations people find themselves in. Openly share your thoughts and ideas on each topic, and, when appropriate, discuss the hope you have in a relationship with Jesus Christ.

BOARD GAME BASH

idea Roll the dice, draw a card, move your playing piece, and enjoy some board games with neighbors. Get out your favorite games, and invite 11 other neighbors for a board game tournament with three tables of four players. Choose games that are played with partners, such as Pictionary and Taboo.

When guests arrive, have them choose partners and a table at which to start. Set a timer for 30 minutes, and begin all the games at the same time. The winners of each game move to a new table. The rest of the players stay where they are. If the timer goes off before a game is finished, the person with the most points or farthest on the game board is the winner of that round.

Continue to play until each game has been played three times or until guests are ready to stop. Give mementos to everybody who played; for instance, you might give everybody a candy bar, bag of coffee beans, or CD of music you compiled electronically.

HELPFUL HINTS

A fun twist on the popular game Scrabble is to play without the board. "Speed Scrabble" starts with each player drawing seven tiles. The person with the letter closest to A says, "Go!" Players should use their own letters to make words horizontally and vertically so that all their letters are used to make words. Players can rearrange their tiles as much as they want to create new words throughout the game, as long as all the words are connected. Players do not play on each other's letters; rather, each player works to use all of his or her own letters.

When a player has used all of his or her letters, he or she says, "draw," and all players must draw another tile. The game continues this way until all the tiles have been drawn and a person has used all his or her tiles. The values of any remaining letters not used in a word count against that player. The values of the letters used in a word count for him or her. At the end of the 30-minute round, the goal is to have the most points possible.

Instant Intentions

Word-based games such as Pictionary or Scattergories often provide opportunities for you to reveal things about your life that wouldn't otherwise come up. Before the game, pray that the Holy Spirit will guide your play and open doors for you to share about your faith. Don't force it, but if you see an opportunity, tell a story about a time God made a difference in your life.

BUNCO

idea Bunco is a simple, fun, and fast-paced game, and a surefire mixer for larger gatherings.

The only catch with Bunco is that you need at least 12 people to play and multiples of four thereafter. So be flexible as the host. You and a friend or two might need to sit out to make sure you have the right number of people. Set up a table for every group of four, and put three dice on each table. You'll also want to give each person a Bunco score sheet (either purchased or just a blank piece of paper) and a pencil. A buzzer or a bell can be used to signal the end of each round. Number the tables from one to four.

> **HELPFUL HINTS**
> No matter what version of Bunco you play, someone who comes to your gathering will know a different version. Try a few variations, and play the one that is most engaging and fun (the reason we chose the "grab the bunco" version for this outreach).

There are numerous versions of Bunco and various score card templates that can easily be found online. The rules to a high-energy version follow. Table one should start each round by ringing the bell. Partners sit across each other at the table. Each person takes turns rolling the three dice. Partners score a point for each die that matches the round (also called the target). For example, during the first round, partners score one point for every "1" they roll. During the second round, partners score one point for every "2" they roll. Partners keep rolling as long as they score at least one point during a roll. When no targets are rolled, the dice go to the next player. When the dice land on three targets (for example, three "3s" in the third round), players yell "Bunco!" All players try to grab the dice. If a player grabs two or more dice, his or her team scores five points and continues rolling. If no one grabs the die, the next player rolls the die, and no points are awarded.

The round is over whenever any pair scores 21 points. The pair with the lower score at table one moves to table four and each player switches partners. The pairs with the highest score at all the other tables move up one table, taking a new partner. Awards can be given for the highest total number of points, the most wins at a table, as well as the total number of "buncos" an individual grabs.

Instant Intentions

Use the natural transition when players switch tables between rounds to spark conversation. You can provide guided questions they should discuss before starting the round that may lead to faith discussions. For example, you could have tables discuss questions like: "Other than family members, what are the three most important things in your life?"

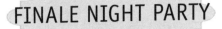

FINALE NIGHT PARTY

idea Television show finales are now a staple of American entertainment, whether it is a reality competition or race, or an action-packed drama. So why not make an event of it, and enjoy it with your neighbors?

Most people are willing to share which television shows they love to watch, and finales are exactly the sorts of shows people are willing to watch with others.

Volunteer your own home for a location if it's suitable. If you don't have enough room for the number of attendees, you might consider another venue, such as a rented clubhouse. Make phone-call invitations, visit door to door, or—if you live in a community with a bulletin board—post an open invitation. Provide plenty to eat, and, if possible, theme the food and the decorations with what you're watching.

Televised competitions usually provide the best kind of group viewing and post-discussion since they have a definitive climax. Competitions can also be especially fun since you can each pick someone to root for. Or, you might hold a contest to see who can guess the ultimate winner. Themed outfits and even themed mini-games aren't out of the question either. Take a cue from the challenges the contestants face on the show for ideas.

This is your opportunity to show your hospitality and spend some time laughing and having fun with your neighbors.

> **HELPFUL HINTS**
> Create a quiz card with questions about the events throughout the show's season, and encourage people to fill these out during your party. If you're watching a travel-related show, you might include a map with colored pins for people to stick into all the countries they've been to. If it's a survival-related show, you could make up a quiz from The Worst-Case Scenario Survival Handbook (or play the game derived from it).

Instant Intentions

Television can sometimes be a source of disagreement between people, and often between Christians and non-Christians. Don't be afraid to explain why you do or do not watch certain shows. Be candid about your decisions, and people will respect you, especially when they experience your love and hospitality during the party. This isn't a good opportunity for pushing your entertainment standards on others, but it may be a good chance to explain your beliefs and the reasons behind them. Make sure to talk about more than just the show during the event, and be sure to ask around to find out what other finales people would like to get together for in the future.

LOVELY LADIES TEA PARTY

idea Help the women in your neighborhood escape from endless errands next Saturday afternoon by hosting an intergenerational, elegant, ladies-only tea.

Begin by delivering invitations to women of all ages in the households near you. To add a personal touch, create handwritten, delicately themed cards with an herbal tea bag attached. On the invitation, request that, if possible, each invitee bring another female relative who is special to her, or a picture of someone special who's not able to attend. Ideas include: mother, daughter, grandmother, granddaughter, aunt, or niece. Explain that this tea will be a relaxing afternoon of ladies-only fun.

HELPFUL HINTS

For extra fun, request that guests come dressed up in lady-like, garden-party finery—dresses, hats, and gloves! Also, if you're expecting young children, set out unbreakable dishes for them to use.

Your tea party menu can be as simple as tiny sandwiches; an assortment of sweets (such as scones and jam); and tea with honey, cream, and sugar. Don't forget to decorate with fresh flowers and elegant dishes; use china, crystal, and silver if you have it. If the weather is nice and you can accommodate the seating, consider holding the party outside on your deck or in your garden.

At the tea party, ask guests to share a story or two about the lady with whom they're attending (or whose picture they've brought). The stories can be humorous, touching, or simply a favorite memory that the women share. These stories will not only encourage further party conversation, but will lead your neighbors past simple surface-level knowledge of each other. Depending on the amount of time you have scheduled, you may also want to plan an activity for the party that all ages would enjoy together, such as decorating picture frames, or baking and decorating sugar cookies.

Instant Intentions

During the tea, you may want to jot down snippets of the stories women share, and use them for conversation-openers in the future. For example, you might say, "I loved your story at the tea party about your beach vacation. Are you planning any upcoming trips this summer?" or "I enjoyed meeting your mom and hearing how she passed along her green thumb to you. Maybe the three of us could go to that new garden shop together…"

MAKE THE MOST OF MOVIE NIGHTS

idea Movie nights with your neighbors aren't just about watching movies. The point is to set up discussions and encourage fellowship—the movies are simply shared experiences and discussion prompts. Here are a few ideas to ensure that the movies and the environment you select are appropriate:

1. *Meet in your home.* When people come into each other's homes, they form a natural bond.

2. *Serve movie food.* Popcorn, chips, pizza, candy, and soda will do it. Ask each group member to bring something to pass around. This ensures that you won't go broke, and it builds ownership of the event. (You *could* also tie your food to the theme of your movie if cost isn't as big of a factor.)

3. *Choose your movies wisely.* As the host, you can decide what to rent. But the video or DVD should be less than 2½ hours long, thought-provoking, and include substantial spiritual and/or emotional content.

4. *Stick with PG or PG-13.* While there will almost always be something in a movie that could offend someone, a PG rating usually ensures that the offense will be minor.

5. *Don't announce the movie's title beforehand.* Some people might decide not to attend because they've already seen the film. But remember, the movie itself isn't the point. Discussion and relationships matter more, so don't reveal the title until plates are full and people are already parked in front of the screen.

6. *The host controls the remote.* This is a matter of respect and resolves a battle before it ever starts.

7. *No pausing.* Once the movie starts, it keeps rolling. That means people

need to plan accordingly for bathroom breaks and soda refills.

8. *The host starts the discussion.* After the movie ends, it's the host's job to get the conversation rolling. The discussion may suddenly take a dramatic turn once it starts, but the first nudge is up to the host.

9. *Don't meet too often.* Keep your movie nights to every month or two. This will keep the event fresh and still allow you to maintain the relationships you're trying to build—especially if you do other activities together.

Instant Intentions

Movies get a bad rap in some circles. But the fact is, they're often both moving and effective in portraying basic truths about us, both humanly and spiritually, in ways that some sermons cannot. So leverage that fact by choosing movies that draw out truths common to everyone.

Use the specific movies in this book to get your movie nights rolling.

Have fun, and watch as the discussions—and friendships—go places you never expected!

MONEY MATTERS

idea Many people today are worried about money. How much is enough for retirement? What can I do about those high-interest credit cards? How can I pay for college? Even those people who know how to put together a budget—and a surprising number of people don't—would like to get a better handle on how to stretch their dollars these days.

Plan an event (or series of events) to teach members of your neighborhood how to handle their finances. Then get the word out! Make your target audience as specific or as broad as you choose (and depending on your selection of presenters). This type of event would be beneficial for single men and women who are just starting out, for teens, or for seniors living on fixed incomes. Tailor your audience to the type of speaker you enlist.

> ### HELPFUL HINTS
> *If you don't personally know a financial expert, pitch your idea to a local accounting or tax service firm. The prospect of obtaining new clients might be enough incentive to have one of the firm's employees serve as the speaker. Another option would be to contact a professor at a college.*

Invite experts who work in the financial world, from within your church or the community, to teach classes on topics such as saving money, getting out of debt, learning about investment strategies, and planning for large purchases.

If you choose to present your event from a Christian perspective, there are prepackaged financial course kits available that explore financial issues from a Christian perspective. Crown Financial Ministries (www.crown.org) and Willow Creek's, Good $ense Ministry (www.goodsenseministry.org) are two such ministries that provide solid financial curricula.

Instant Intentions

The topic of tithing may come up at this event. Or if it doesn't, bring it up yourself! It's a great way to talk about biblical issues in a natural setting.

MOVIE NIGHT

idea What better way to spark lively and deep conversation about social and moral issues than to watch movies together?

Invite some neighbors over for a movie and discussion. Choose a movie with many possible discussion elements. The film doesn't have to be a serious drama or contain a deep, hard-hitting theme. In fact, comedies or family movies are powerful springboards for great conversation. Also, young parents would appreciate a night out, without leaving their children at home. If the children do not watch the movie with the rest of the group, you might collect money from everyone to hire a babysitter, then show a kids' movie in another room of the house.

Obtain a copy of the movie in time for your event. Research your movie choice ahead of time to develop some meaningful questions. Pop up some popcorn, and chill the sodas. Let the movie begin. And when *The End* fades out on screen, be ready to explore the deeper meaning of the movie. Talk about such things as the motivation of characters; the humor found in the plot; personal consequence of actions; and any depictions of redemption, love, hope, forgiveness, or transformation.

> **HELPFUL HINTS**
>
> *Use Group's Dinner and a Movie to help plan your event. Even if you don't use the entire plan for each movie, you will find many helpful ideas to make your movie night a hit. Each movie featured in the book includes a story synopsis, ratings information, activities or trivia about the movie or actors, and discussion questions. And if you choose to make a more extravagant event to include a meal, you can even find theme dinner menus with recipes and decorating ideas.*

Explore the basic themes portrayed in the film, and discuss how each of you might connect the movie to your life and world.

Instant Intentions

Prepare a specific question or two ahead of time that might launch conversation about God, faith, or spirituality. Be sure to think through or even write out what your response would be to your question so that you are well-prepared to share. However, if you're just getting to know your neighbors, the topic of faith might not come up so quickly. If the discussion does not ever touch specifically on faith, that's OK. Your active participation and insights will set the stage for future opportunities to talk about your faith in Christ—especially in one-on-one discussions.

MOVIE 1

idea *Good Night, and Good Luck* (2005)

Genre: Drama
Length: 93 minutes
Rating: PG for mild thematic elements and brief language
Plot: CBS journalist Edward R. Murrow and producer Fred Friendly take a stand against Senator Joseph McCarthy's anti-communist crusade in the 1950s. Murrow's broadcasts begin McCarthy's public and political downhill slide, but the battle inflicts wounds on both sides. The shows begin to alienate advertisers, and as CBS begins to lose profits, Murrow's boss finds himself caught between the need for integrity in television news and the need for corporate sponsorship.

DISCUSSION STARTER QUESTIONS:

- Do you agree with how Murrow and Friendly went about their jobs in this film? Explain.

- How do you explain the culture of fear that developed during the McCarthy era? What similarities, if any, do you see in our culture today?

- How do you think our society should respond to people whose values differ from ours? How should we respond as individuals?

- In your opinion, what is the responsibility of the media in our everyday lives? What impact does the media have on our way of thinking?

- What is the power of the spoken word in our world? How is it demonstrated in this film? How have you seen it demonstrated in your own life?

MOVIE 2

idea *Dreamer* (2005)

Genre: Drama/Family/Sport
Length: 106 minutes
Rating: PG for brief mild language
Plot: This movie, inspired by a true story, focuses primarily on Ben Crane and his daughter, Cale. Ben trains racehorses and seldom has much time for his daughter, who loves horses herself. When something appears to be wrong with a prize filly before a race, Ben tells the owner not to race her. When he does and the filly falls and breaks her leg, the owner fires Ben and gives him the horse in lieu of wages. Against all odds, Ben and Cale, with the help of Ben's father, nurse the horse—and their own relationship—back to health.

DISCUSSION STARTER QUESTIONS:

- What was Cale's relationship with her father like at the beginning of the movie? What was it like at the end?
- What was Ben's relationship with his father like at the beginning of the movie? What was it like at the end?
- What caused the changes in these relationships?
- Describe a relationship in your own life where healing took place. What did it take for it to begin healing?
- What else can we learn from this movie about the importance of family?

MOVIE 3

idea *Walk the Line* (2005)

Genre: Drama

Length: 136 minutes

Rating: PG-13 for some language, thematic material, and depiction of drug dependency

Plot: Growing up in Arkansas, Johnny Cash had a close relationship with his older brother and an interest in music. But when his brother dies in a freak accident, Johnny develops a sense of guilt and deep pain from the loss. As soon as he's old enough, Johnny escapes into the Army, where he's able to travel, and he learns to play the guitar and experiment with song writing.

When he returns to the States, he attempts to settle into a normal life. He marries, gets a job as a salesman, has kids, and forms a local band—which is discovered by the legendary Sam Phillips. He goes on several tours with Elvis and Jerry Lee Lewis, among others. It is not long, though, before Johnny's marriage falls apart.

During this time, he also meets and tours with his childhood idol June Carter. It is not until June and her devout Christian parents help Cash overcome his addictions, that he slowly begins to straighten out.

DISCUSSION STARTER QUESTIONS:

- What particularly struck you about Johnny Cash's life? What aspects of the relationship between Johnny and June caught your attention?
- How did Johnny's relationship with his dad impact him throughout his life? Is it possible for a person to find healing from such painful, dysfunctional relationships? Explain.
- Why do you think June Carter and her parents decided to help Johnny? What do you think motivated their kindness and commitment to him?
- Why do you think music was such an attraction for Cash? What is it about music that you find appealing?

MOVIE 4

idea *Everything Is Illuminated* (2005)

Genre: Adventure/Comedy/Drama

Length: 106 minutes

Rating: PG-13 for some disturbing images, violence, sexual content, and language

Plot: Jonathan is a quiet, large-spectacled Jewish American known as "The Collector" because he accumulates bits and pieces of his life and stores them in Ziploc bags. He goes on a search to find the woman who saved his grandfather during World War II, in a Ukrainian village that had been obliterated by the Nazis.

With the guide of a cranky grandfather and his overenthusiastic grandson Alex—whose near-constant stream of twisted English only makes matters more difficult—Jonathan begins his uncomfortable and annoying trek. But what starts out as a farcical journey turns meaningful, as the past—and increasingly astounding revelations about it—begins to emerge.

DISCUSSION STARTER QUESTIONS:

- What do you think Jonathan is really searching for? What are Alex and his grandfather searching for? What does each character find?
- What do you think of Alex's grandfather's attitude toward the Ukrainian Jews? What do you think fuels that attitude? How does it change as the movie progresses?
- How responsible are we for the evil that happens in the world? Should we feel guilty for others' actions—especially actions done by those we know personally? Why or why not?
- How does the humor in the movie make it more (or less) poignant, once the truth has been discovered? Did you find this movie more hopeful or tragic? Explain.
- What do think is meant by this movie's title—*Everything Is Illuminated*? *Is* it? Why or why not?

MOVIE 5

idea *Crimes and Misdemeanors* (1989)

Genre: Comedy/Drama
Length: 107 minutes
Rating: PG-13 for language and some sexuality
Plot: Doctor Judah Rosenthal is a successful man—he has a good family and a respectable and profitable career. However, he is trapped in an ongoing affair with Dolores. When she gives him an ultimatum—marriage or full disclosure—he is faced with a crisis: He can do the right thing and come clean, risking his "perfect" life, or he can bury his dark secret in murder and go on living as if everything were normal.

Meanwhile, filmmaker Cliff Stern, whose marriage is also on the rocks, is forced into directing a film that goes against his artistic sensibilities. While his marriage and career are falling apart, he begins to pursue Halley Reed, a film producer. Both men face desperation but address their problems in very different ways—with strikingly different results.

DISCUSSION STARTER QUESTIONS:

- How do the two main characters in the film view life? How does a person's view of life affect his or her actions?
- What different views concerning morality are offered in this film? Do they reflect our culture's views on the subject? Why or why not?
- Is it ever possible to really escape from our problems? Do you think Judah was able to escape? Why or why not?
- Is justice something we should expect in this life? How should we respond to injustice in the world?
- Do you think moral values are objective or subjective? Why?
- What are the major moral dilemmas that people face today? How should we respond to them?

MOVIE 6

idea *Glory Road* (2006)

Genre: Drama/Sport
Length: 106 minutes
Rating: PG for racial issues including violence and epithets, and momentary language
Plot: This movie is based on a true story. Don Haskins, a girls basketball coach, is hired to become the men's basketball coach of the Texas Western Miners. He goes on the recruiting trail to find the best talent in the land, black *or* white—in the mid-'60s, when black and white were seldom mixed anywhere, let alone on a college basketball court.

The team Haskins puts together—seven black players and five white—is repeatedly ridiculed and threatened as they travel around the country. And yet, Haskins and his Miners come together as a team and reach the NCAA championship game against perennial powerhouse Kentucky.

DISCUSSION STARTER QUESTIONS:

- What risks did Haskins and his coaches take in recruiting black players at that time? What risks did the players themselves—both black *and* white—take in accepting Haskins' offer?
- Besides their accomplishments as a team, what other advances did you see both on the court and off because of the team Haskins put together?
- Why was it difficult for the coaches and players to listen and learn from each other? What can you learn from this?
- What kind of people do you struggle most with seeing as equals? How would seeing them through God's eyes change your relationships?
- What kind of risk might you be called to take right now? What do you think your first step is in accepting that challenge?

NASCAR RACE DAY

idea If you want to do something different to catch the attention of people in your neighborhood, *here's* an event to try!

Contrary to common perceptions, NASCAR fans come from all levels of society—and they will be pleasantly surprised to have you tailor an event to their interests.

A month or more in advance, check the NASCAR Nextel Cup Series schedule (www.nascar.com/races), and determine a race that you'd like to show on a big screen for race fans in your neighborhood. Be sure you have a good video projector, screen, sound system, and TV hookup for the right channel. (An outdoor showing would be even more fun, but daylight may make it impossible to get a good image from the projector.)

> **HELPFUL HINTS**
>
> *Invite your neighbors to wear their favorite drivers' numbers. Place checkered flags on your lawn as decorations. And for kids who may get bored by the real race, show the children's movie* Cars *in another room.*

If you can possibly use an area of your church, your neighbors may well be intrigued that a church would promote such an event on church grounds.

Spread the word by handing out fliers. You could also put up posters in neighborhood parks and restaurants.

Plan and advertise free refreshments. (You might want to make it clear in all advertising that you'll allow no alcoholic beverages.) Even if attendance at your event isn't overwhelming, people in your neighborhood will begin to catch the idea that your interests may not be as ordinary as they thought!

Instant Intentions

Before your NASCAR neighbors head home, ask if anyone would be interested in helping the kids in your neighborhood build go-carts. That way, you can sponsor your own race day—and build cars and relationships at the same time!

NEIGHBORHOOD CRAFT NIGHT

idea Invite all your neighborhood crafters over to work on their favorite craft, socialize, and get to know one another better.

At the first get-together, work out the details. Choose a standing night when you'll meet, either monthly or bimonthly. Determine if you want to rotate or always meet at one house. Also, decide if the host will provide snacks or if everyone will bring something to share.

Explain that the event is for any kind of crafter who would enjoy crafting while sitting side by side with others who value the process of creativity. Perhaps a certain period of time during each meeting can be devoted to a particular artist teaching an aspect of his or her craft. For example, this would be a great time for scrapbookers to bring along and share their punches and scissors with one another. Or, needle or bead crafters can bring along samples of finished projects to show off. Children can bring their favorite coloring or sticker books and join in the fun. This is a great way to take a secluded activity and make it a wonderful social event!

> **HELPFUL HINTS**
>
> *If you know someone who has meaningful photos—perhaps an elderly person who lives far from loved ones—but who is unable to organize them, offer to put the pictures together in a memory album as a gift. Then invite other crafters or scrapbookers from your neighborhood to help you put together a beautiful album for the senior to enjoy. Not only will you bless the owner of the photos, but creating such a kind gift may generate opportunities for significant conversation with that person—and those helping you.*

Instant Intentions

Listen to your guests as they visit around the work area. What is important to them? What gives them hope? What is of concern or exciting for them? Learn to listen well so you can understand in deeper ways what is going on in your neighbors' hearts. Then, as opportunities arise, you can ask them about those significant things.

PAMPER YOURSELF PARTY

idea Invite some neighbor ladies over for a pamper party complete with facials, foot soaks, and manicures! This kind of party would work best in the evening to promote true relaxation. Send out invitations for your party, describing the evening. Let ladies know to dress comfortably.

It's important to create a very relaxing atmosphere for this kind of party. Set the mood in your home by dimming the lights, placing several lit candles around the room, and playing some soft instrumental music.

You can either purchase premade facial masks in the health and beauty department of a store or create some homemade treatments. You can set thin slices of cucumber or warm-water-soaked chamomile tea bags on eyelids. (Just be sure to squeeze out excess water before placing the tea bags over the eyes.)

> **HELPFUL HINTS**
> *Paraffin wax kits can be found at most department stores for about $30. Add a little extra pampering to your party by letting your guests take a warm and fragrant hand dip.*

Mash up bananas for a great facial mask, and soak feet in tubs or large bowls of warm water. Place a bunch of marbles at the bottom of the tubs to roll feet around on for a wonderful massage. Have a variety of nail polish colors, polish remover, cotton balls, files, and clippers.

Set up three different stations for the three different treatments. One will be the facial and eye treatment. One will be the foot soak, and one will be the manicure. As guests arrive, assign them a place to start, spreading them out so that each station has an equal number of people. Have guests rotate through at 5- to 10-minute intervals.

Instant Intentions

Play instrumental praise and worship for your background music. Allow conversation to happen naturally during this time; you might talk about other ways each of you needs pampering, comfort, or relief in life. Discuss ways you can help each other in the future; for instance, make plans to go to a spa or even get away for a weekend night.

SEEKERS' STUDY

idea There are many subjects seekers have interest in today, and offering a Bible study to some of your friends who are unchurched might be just the way to share your faith. You only need a few people for a study like this—maybe even just you and one other couple.

Share in the context of your home. Invite a couple in the neighborhood over for a study. Of course, you want to have built enough of a relationship with them to know their interests. In thinking about doing this, you might ask some leading questions: "Have you ever thought about sitting down and talking through some of the issues the Bible raises?" "If you could ask any question about Jesus or the Bible, what would it be?" Or, "How about sitting down with us some night and talking about spiritual things like the Bible? Would you be interested?"

> **HELPFUL HINTS**
> *Take it slow. Don't try to push people into a deep spiritual discussion they're not ready to have. At the same time, remember that most people have a spiritual interest, even if it isn't yet in Christianity. With the right questions, you can explore that interest in a way that leads to a deeper discussion about spiritual things.*

Serve refreshments to engender a warm atmosphere, and have comfortable seating so people feel at home. If someone brings up an idea that goes against God's Word, couch your responses openly but not condemningly. Just stick to the facts. People will appreciate both your candor and your acceptance of them, and through your transparency they will catch a glimpse of who Jesus is.

Instant Intentions

Some people may think that if they don't become Christians, you'll reject them as friends. Make sure they know that's not the case. But also let them know you'll be praying for them and hoping for other opportunities to talk about the importance of your faith in your own life.

SENIOR STORY SOURCE

idea Children love stories, and elderly people are a great source for stories like no other! However, many children and their grandparents don't live in nearby communities. Build the connection between generations in your neighborhood by facilitating a story time between kids and those who've been around the block a few more times.

Arrange regular meeting times for seniors to spend time with children to read and tell stories. Monthly or weekly gathering times, with a different storyteller each time, will allow the children opportunity to hear from a wide variety of storytellers. Use your home or a community building, if possible.

Ask your seniors to start by reading aloud a select story on a subject that corresponds with additional real-life stories they can share with the group. For example, the storyteller might read *Mike Mulligan and His Steam Shovel*, then relate his own experiences working as a construction worker 50 years ago and what life and his job were like during that time.

> ### HELPFUL HINTS
> *There are many resources available from the library, bookstore, national organizations, and online sources to help teach about the process of storytelling. Connect your storytellers with any support they may need or find helpful.*

A question-and-answer time after the stories is a good way for children to explore ideas and learn more about the seniors, their lives, and their times.

Instant Intentions

If a senior has to cancel a story time due to ill health, use it as an opportunity to brighten the senior's day *and* teach kids about caring. When you call all of the children in the story group to let them know of the cancellation, ask them to come over to make and sign a get-well card for the senior.

TOURNAMENT-STYLE FUN

idea Host a low-pressure pool, foosball, or darts tournament in your own home. This is an exciting way for the men in your neighborhood to get to know each other without the strain of just sitting and talking.

To begin, pick an upcoming date when you would be able to host. One idea is to pick a date when a local professional sports team is playing a televised game; show the game during your event to provide background interest. Next, personally contact your neighbors, and invite them to come. Let them know that there is no great skill required—this will just be for fun. Your tournament will run the most smoothly if you invite people in multiples of two so that no one has to sit out of the action.

> **HELPFUL HINTS**
> *Have plenty of snacks and drinks available to keep your guests comfortable. Consider setting up a white board for players to keep track of the bracket or to keep score on.*

In order to facilitate new interactions and conversations between your neighbors, pick teams by a random method such as drawing names out of a hat. Then, set up a simple tournament bracket that allows every team to play every other team. Also make sure that each team gets to play more than once.

If you have more than one game in your home (such as a foosball table *and* a dartboard), you should make the non-bracketed activity an "open game" so that everyone has another option to continue playing when he or she isn't involved in the tournament table. You might also consider setting up a card or board game for others to play.

Instant Intentions

Take this opportunity to try to get to know what your neighbors are truly interested in. Then follow up with another social invitation at a later date. For example, if you learn that one of your neighbors loves to golf, invite him to play a round at the local course with you—and call other neighbors to join in.

WEEKLY WATCH

idea Here's an idea for people who anticipate the upcoming new episodes of their television favorites—host a weekly watching party in your home.

To get started, have a quick face-to-face conversation with your neighbors and mention that you'd like to start a "TV night" at your house. Ask if they'd be interested in joining you, and, if so, find out what some of their favorite TV shows are. Compile a list of the responses you get, then pick the most popular night and time for your neighbors to gather at your house. Have another conversation with your neighbors to let them know the night and time you'll be meeting. Let them know that they are free to come each week or just when they can—it's not a formal event requiring an RSVP.

On TV night, consider upping the entertainment factor by taking a weekly poll on what next week's episode will include, what decision a certain character will make, and so on. If your group is watching a reality show, consider picking teams to pretend to join, and advocate which decisions your team should make next. Or try picking and rooting for certain individual characters to see who comes closest to making it to the finals. Provide a light snack for your guests each week; food has a way of making people a bit more comfortable!

> ### HELPFUL HINTS
> *Offer to record shows for neighbors if they can't make it over for that week's episode. Lend the videotape, or let people know when they can come over by themselves to watch the program on TiVo. If you have people joining you who are new to a show, do your best as a group to catch them up with the characters and plot line so they can enjoy watching as much as you do.*

The idea of this weekly event is just to relax and enjoy your neighbors' company. Over time, your group's conversations will grow beyond the television shows, moving to deeper topics as you get to know each other better.

Instant Intentions

While you're watching the show together, take private note of any personal tidbits about your neighbors—from how they respond to the characters, situations, or even other viewers. Use your observations to strike up a conversation with that person later on. For example, you could say, "I noticed how we both laughed hysterically at the Smiths' fishing adventure last week. I've had some great times on the lake with my brother. Do you happen to fish?" Maybe even take that next step and invite your neighbor on your upcoming fishing trip.

WOMEN ENCOURAGEMENT PARTNERS

idea As women go through the seasons of life, they meet many challenges. They need other women who have passed through each season to encourage and sometimes advise them. An encouragement partner can relate her experiences—successes *and* failures—at different stages and in different circumstances of life. She can testify to God's presence and help through it all and can describe lessons she learned from the tough times. An encouragement partner could listen to the woman in need, pray with her, and discuss options.

Four groups to consider targeting are newlyweds, new moms, moms of teens, and women approaching menopause. Find several trustworthy women in your church who would be willing to be mentors. You might ask your pastoral staff to suggest names. Explain that the program is not designed to be an overtly Christian service, but is more of a way to help others and build relationships that hopefully will lead to a deeper spiritual understanding of Jesus and his love.

> **HELPFUL HINTS**
>
> *Depending on the number of interested parties, you may need to adjust your program accordingly. For example, if you start small, you may be able to offer one-on-one mentor relationships. But if you have a large number of women interested in a certain topic or stage of life, it may make more sense to have regular round-table meetings.*

Once you have your mentors, announce your idea to the neighborhood, and ask women who would be interested in meeting with an encouraging mentor to sign up. Explain the purpose of the program, and plan a kick-off meeting. Also, inform ladies that this ministry is limited in time—for example, that it will meet twice a month for six months.

Kick off your program with a continental breakfast for your mentors. Showcase biblical examples of encouragement and advice, such as Ruth and Naomi, or contemporary examples from someone's personal experience. Explain the ground rules. Include subjects such as confidentiality and faithfulness in meeting. Next, take the women who have expressed interest in meeting with a mentor, and with a great deal of prayer, match up each participating woman with a mentor.

The mentors will be able to help women work through whatever stage of life they're experiencing, and more important, as relationships deepen, to show other women how to become grounded in a relationship with God.

Instant Intentions

This sort of mentoring program is a perfect opportunity for a Christian woman to testify to God's presence and help through the seasons of life, especially the lessons learned from the tough times.

HOLIDAYS AND SEASONAL CELEBRATIONS

*"Always be full of joy
in the Lord.
I say it again—rejoice!"*

PHILIPPIANS 4:4

The Fourth of July. Thanksgiving. Christmas. All special times that people share in common. Why not actually *share* those special times with your neighbors?

A holiday is the perfect time to reach out to your neighbors because, due to media coverage and advertisements, everyone is conscious of the upcoming event. Use this shared experience as an ice breaker and a friend maker.

The ideas in this chapter can help you to easily incorporate new friendships and new traditions into any holiday season. Get ready to celebrate!

AUTUMN FESTIVAL

idea As an alternative to Halloween or just as a great excuse for a party, celebrate fall with your neighbors by hosting an autumn festival. Single neighbors, families with older kids, and the elderly can all be involved. Explain that there will be fun and food for everybody, as well as the opportunity to give the neighborhood children a holiday to remember. Enlist neighbors to help with setting up a child-friendly celebration in your living or family room, basement, or back yard.

<table>
<tr><td>

HELPFUL HINTS

For added fun, throw down some hay for a real festival feel, and play some hoedown-style country music in the background. You may want to enlist adults to be in charge of each station, especially with face painting and pie throwing.

</td></tr>
</table>

Aim for a fun festival experience; create booths from fold-out card tables covered with old cloth. Offer face-painting, water balloon popping, and pie-throwing activities. Put down tarps or old sheets to protect flooring if you're indoors, and let the children have some fun. Offer each child a goodie bag complete with caramel apples and candy. Encourage all the adults of the neighborhood to supervise and engage in the activities while enjoying great conversation at the same time.

Instant Intentions

While the children enjoy themselves in a safe and fun environment, take the time to meet each parent and strike up a conversation. This activity will provide plenty to talk about even when the event is over. Make sure to thank the volunteers by sending a thank-you note with some homemade cookies or other treats.

CHRISTMAS TEA

idea As this special season draws near, take the time to invite the women of your neighborhood into your home for an afternoon of conversation and tasty treats.

Create a respite from this busy season by hosting a Christmas tea. Depending on your neighborhood size and home accommodations, this may be a large or small event. Hand-deliver invitations, and make sure you personally invite each woman.

No formal presentation is needed, but take the time to search the Internet for a special seasonal sweet such as scones and clotted creams or homemade breads. Spread your table with festive plates and linens, light a few candles, and play some Christmas music to create a warm and inviting environment.

Your guests will love an afternoon away from the hectic schedule that Christmastime can bring. Pour some tea, and engage in friendly conversation while getting to know the women who live near you.

> **HELPFUL HINTS**
> *Delight your guests with peppermint bark, a favorite Christmas treat.*
>
> *Hammer candy canes in a plastic bag into ¼-inch chunks, to yield 1 cup.*
>
> *Then melt 2 pounds of white chocolate in a double boiler. Combine candy-cane chunks with chocolate. Pour mixture onto a cookie sheet layered with waxed paper, and place in the refrigerator for 45 minutes. Break up and serve with tea!*

Instant Intentions

An afternoon of tea and sweets is sure to yield a personal connection you didn't have before. Within a week after the tea, set a future lunch date with one or two women with whom you felt the greatest connection. By establishing this commitment right away, a meaningful relationship will have a greater chance of developing.

CHRISTMAS WRAP-UP

idea As Christmas approaches, everybody seems to be in a crunch to get presents wrapped and cards signed and addressed. Use this opportunity to gather with neighbors and get the job done together.

Invite neighbors with a simple phone call or hand-delivered note, informing them of the party's time and date. Let them know you will supply wrapping paper, tape, and scissors.

On the day of the party, prepare a table with gift-wrapping supplies. Have coffee, tea, or hot cider and a light snack to serve your guests. Play some soft Christmas music in the background for a festive atmosphere.

HELPFUL HINTS

Have some fancy pens, bows, ribbons, and other decorations available for guests to give their cards and gifts an extra-special touch.

Facilitate an inexpensive gift exchange during your party. Set a $5 limit. Ornaments, candles, lotion, or coffee mugs are some examples of things most people enjoy. For the exchange, give each person a number to hold and a different number to put on the gift. Then have each person find the gift that matches his or her number.

Instant Intentions

Sometime during the party, ask your guests to share how they celebrate Christmas. Be ready to share how you celebrate—with the focus on Jesus.

EASTER-EGG HUNT

idea Reach out to your neighbors with this springtime classic. Recruit two or three neighbors—perhaps seniors, singles, or teenagers—to help you buy candy and plastic eggs. Then spend an afternoon together filling the eggs with the candy. Decide on the place to have your hunt, whether it's a close-by park or a neighbor's large yard.

Send out notes or cards to your neighbors with small children, inviting them to the hunt. You will want to hold the hunt on the weekend before Easter so there is plenty of opportunity for you to invite your unchurched neighbors to your church's Easter service.

An hour or so before the hunt, meet with the neighbors who are helping you hide the eggs. Rope off a small section for toddlers to collect their eggs scattered on the ground. Hide the rest of the eggs around the remainder of the park or yard. Consider keeping a list of where the eggs are and how many you're hiding. This will come in handy later.

As neighbors arrive, keep children together in an area away from the eggs. Make sure every child has a basket or sack to collect his or her eggs. Allow children under 3 to go first and find their eggs in the roped-off section. When they are finished, the older children can search for the harder-to-find eggs. Make sure all the eggs are found by the end of the event.

> **HELPFUL HINTS**
>
> *Provide extra eggs to give to kids who have trouble finding any. Also, you may want to include gift certificates for ice cream or fast food in the eggs. Or, hide a "golden egg" with a more valuable prize of either money or a gift certificate to a toy store.*
>
> *Have a potluck lunch after the egg hunt to further your connection with your neighbors.*

Instant Intentions

Make it your goal to invite at least one family to your church's Easter service. Have a backup plan if the family says no or has other plans. Also invite a family over for Easter dinner.

GINGERBREAD HOUSES

idea The Christmas season is always a great time to gather with neighbors and experience a fun craft. Ring in the holiday season with children and adults alike by decorating gingerbread houses.

Use whole graham crackers for the two sidewalls and roof of the house, and half graham crackers for the front and back walls. "Glue" them together with royal icing. Here's the recipe:

Royal Icing

This recipe is for a single batch. You will probably need several, but if you make them all at once, keep them in separate bowls. Royal Icing dries very quickly and is like cement. Keep it well covered.

- 3 egg whites
- 1½ teaspoons cream of tartar
- 3½ cups confectioners sugar

In a large bowl, beat the egg whites until they begin to foam. Add the cream of tartar, and beat until the whites are stiff but not dry. Gradually beat in the confectioners sugar, beating for about five minutes until it reaches spreading consistency. Keep it covered, and refrigerate until needed.

Using the frosting as glue, decorate your houses with all sorts of candies, cookies, pretzels, and sprinkles. Let your imaginations go wild.

As you create these gingerbread houses with your neighbors, talk about your lives. Ask everyone to share a favorite holiday tradition from his or her childhood—or one the person would like to begin. Afterward, have everyone take a gingerbread house home. Or, you may decide to deliver the houses to other neighbors as gifts.

Instant Intentions

Play some Christ-centered Christmas music in the background as you create the gingerbread houses. Pray for an opportunity to discuss the meaning behind the lyrics of these songs.

HELPFUL HINTS

Instead of using graham crackers, use real gingerbread for an extra-special treat.

GINGERBREAD DOUGH

- 1 cup butter at room temperature
- 1¾ cups brown sugar
- 1¼ cups white sugar
- 2 tablespoons molasses
- 6 eggs
- 6 cups all-purpose flour
- 2 teaspoons baking soda
- 1 tablespoon ground ginger
- 1 tablespoon ground cinnamon
- 1 tablespoon allspice

Preheat your oven to 325 degrees. Line several cookie sheets with aluminum foil. Butter and flour the foil. In a large bowl, cream the butter and sugars. Beat in the molasses and eggs. In another large bowl, sift dry ingredients. Combine mixtures and knead into a smooth ball. Cover and refrigerate at least 30 minutes.

On a well-floured surface, roll out a small amount of the dough until it is ¼-inch thick. For each house you make, cut out two rectangles that are 4x4-inch, two that are 4x6-inch and two that are 4x8-inch. Using the spatula, lift the dough and place it on the prepared cookie sheet.

Bake for 15 to 20 minutes or until the dough is slightly firm. Let it cool on racks until firm enough to handle. Peel the foil off the sections, and set the pieces aside to dry thoroughly overnight.

Use the icing like glue to assemble your houses. The 4x6-inch rectangles are your two sidewalls, the 4-inch squares are front and back and the 4x8-inch rectangles form the roof. After you've assembled the walls of your house, let it dry for about 30 minutes before assembling your roof.

HALLOWEEN ALTERNATIVE

idea Halloween can be a difficult holiday to maneuver for many people who live in your neighborhood. If you're looking for an alternative that allows you to stay at home and still be involved with your neighbors, here's a great idea. It will bring you closer to your neighbors and give you the opportunity to be a light on a dark night.

Start by making an autumn treat for each of your neighbors, such as an autumn tea mix or a plate of cookies. Attach invitation cards to each treat, and, before it gets dark, deliver them to all of your neighbors. The invitation card should repeat your verbal invitation to your home at about 8 or 8:30 p.m. for hot cider and pie. Make sure you include your name, address, and phone number.

> **HELPFUL HINTS**
> *If neighbors are interested, encourage them to bring a pie or other dessert of their own to share. Many neighbors are more likely to come if they are allowed to contribute.*

As you deliver your invitations, you may discover you have elderly neighbors who live alone. Invite them to spend the evening with your family helping you prepare pie and hot cider.

Set up tables for your neighbors to sit around and talk and enjoy a hot cup of cider and slice of pie. You'll be amazed at the relationships that develop around this fellowship experience. If you are consistent, this will become an event your neighbors look forward to!

Instant Intentions

Don't be discouraged if only a small number of neighbors show up the first time you host this Halloween alternative. Persistence is the key to relationships that lead to opportunities to talk about Jesus with your neighbors. If you have made a neighborhood map, (see page 38) this event is an excellent opportunity to learn more about your neighbors and pray for them specifically. As you pray, God will give you more ideas of how to serve them and build deeper relationships.

HALLOWEEN HANDOUTS

idea On Halloween evening, accomplish the unexpected as you go out trick-or-treating—by giving treats *to* your neighbors instead.

Go house to house, offering candies, snacks, or candles attached to a ribbon and a note. On your note say something like, "It's no trick! We're your neighbors, and we'd like to get to know you!" Include your name, address, e-mail, and phone number if you wish.

Jot down the addresses of the houses where you trick or treat, and stop by during the following week to say hello.

Instant Intentions

Follow-up prayers, notes of encouragement, and phone calls can go a long way in developing deep relationships with your neighbors. Don't forget to follow up!

HELPFUL HINTS

You'll discover that giving treats softens hearts. If you ask your neighbors if they have any needs you can pray for, many will respond positively. Use sensitivity in deciding when to ask. But if you do ask, take time to jot down prayer requests, along with names, addresses, and, if they're willing to share, phone numbers. Ask permission to share these requests with others if you plan on doing so, and also be sure to ask if you can contact them for updates.

LIGHT UP YOUR NEIGHBORHOOD

idea This is a way to make annual winter decorating more interesting and more fun.

Send an invitation to your neighbors to put up their Christmas decorations together on the same day. Send a letter around the neighborhood suggesting that you all get together on a Saturday to prepare for the holidays. Mail it just before Thanksgiving in the form of a Christmas card for a December 1 decorating date. Tell them that it will begin with coffee and pastries at your house for a good chance to get to know the neighborhood. Promise that many hands make light work!

HELPFUL HINTS

If your neighbors agree to light the neighborhood with candles, you will need to supply a pile of sand, white paper bags (about the size of school lunch sacks), and candles. Fill each bag a quarter full with sand, place the candle inside, fold the edges of the sack outward, and light the candle. It creates a beautiful effect in the evenings.

You might be more likely to get a response if you offer to help. Mention that you have a ladder or staple gun that will be available on that day.

A nice touch would be to set up bagged candles along the street, lining the whole neighborhood.

Instant Intentions

Another obvious chance for a get-together would be a time to take down the decorations. Make sure to take time while you are decorating to get to know your neighbors. Ask them questions about how their family likes to celebrate the holidays and whether or not they have any family traditions. Ask about the history of the neighborhood and how long people have lived there. Ask if there might be someone in the neighborhood who is unable to decorate his or her own house and might want help.

Afterward, invite everyone over to your house to make Christmas cookies.

MAY DAY BASKETS

idea Very few things in life are free or come without strings attached. Your neighbors will welcome the beauty of spring on May Day with a homemade basket filled with spring flowers and sweet treats.

Cut a triangle shape out of brightly colored construction paper. Make the point flat and the long edge rounded. Roll the triangle into a cone, and glue or tape the two sides together. Make a handle by stapling or taping a 12-inch strip of construction paper or ribbon to opposite sides of the top of the cone basket. Fill your cone basket with real or homemade flowers and candy.

After you've made the baskets and filled them, hang them on your neighbors' doors and get away without being noticed.

Instant Intentions

Say a short prayer, asking God to show you who to bless with the May Day baskets. Use this opportunity to talk to your neighbors (if they discover you're the giver) about gifts; discuss the best gift you've ever received or given. If appropriate, share about the gift of forgiveness you've received from God.

HELPFUL HINTS

Buy straw or plastic baskets from the dollar store, and fill them with homemade cookies or muffins. Unlike the cone basket, a store-bought basket will also be able to sit on a porch for your neighbors who don't have doorknobs to hang things from.

Many people nowadays rarely use their front doors and enter their homes through the garage. So be sure to have the basket deliverer ring the doorbell when the basket is hung. Be waiting in your car for the basket deliverer's quick getaway.

MOTHER'S DAY DINNER

idea Men are good at many things, but remembering holidays…well, let's just say that sometimes a reminder can be helpful. You can help make that reminder into a special night for everyone in your neighborhood.

Have the men in your neighborhood plan a Mother's Day dinner for the special women in their lives. You could also turn this into a multigenerational celebration—get the kids involved with helping; invite the grandmothers, and honor them as well. If there are singles in your neighborhood, ask them to invite their moms. If you have neighbors who can't bring anyone, invite them to come and share special stories of their moms.

> ### HELPFUL HINTS
> *If one of your men is particularly gifted with video software, let him create a video or slide show of the wives and mothers you're honoring. It could be a powerful time watching it together at the end of your evening.*

But make sure the dads are in charge. This is an opportunity for them to use their creative abilities without blowing their masculine cover, and it will allow those with the gift of administration to use it somewhere other than work, a house project, or the budget. Work with one or more of the men to pull the plan together and get everything assigned. There's probably at least one cook among your men—let him have at it. And buy flowers—c'mon guys, it's Mother's Day.

Throw in some games, too. One fun idea would be to take turns blindfolding Mom, letting everyone shout at once, and having her try to find her "child" amidst the din (even if it's the child she married!).

Instant Intentions

As you see families interact and as people share memories of Mom, you may notice situations that need prayer and assistance. After the event, tactfully address any areas where you think you might be able to help, whether it's someone who is lonely away from family, or a family with special needs. In all cases, pray!

NATIONAL NIGHT OUT

idea Many cities in America schedule a national night out in the summertime and make many resources available so neighbors can have an exciting and safe neighborhood get-together. You could be the catalyst for an easy party your neighbors will be talking about for a long time.

First, call your city's chamber of commerce to see if they are part of a national neighborhood night out, or if they have scheduled their own citywide event. On that evening, many cities will send their emergency personnel (such as firefighters, paramedics, and police officers) to your neighborhood to tell your children all about their jobs. Some cities even provide a small amount of cash to buy supplies and send a "party van" that provides activities for the children at your party. Neighbors who know each other create safer neighborhoods, so most cities are eager to reward neighborhoods that get together for this kind of celebration.

If your city doesn't make provisions for a night like this, don't hesitate to call your local fire department or police department and ask if they would reserve some personnel for the event you are planning. Most departments are more than happy to come and spend time with the families on your block, talking about how they serve the community and showing off their equipment and vehicles (this is exciting for children!). If you are really ambitious, go to www.nationalnightout.org/nno, and request

HELPFUL HINTS

Don't make the mistake of doing it all! Neighbors are more likely to participate when they can contribute. Share the work with everybody. Even if they say no, just asking people begins a relationship. And it's all about relationships!

If members from your church do help take care of the neighborhood children, remind them not to turn this into an evangelistic event. As long as they do a really good job of providing entertainment for the children, you'll have plenty of great opportunities for meaningful spiritual conversations. Your neighbors will be more apt to listen to the truth about Jesus from someone like you, whom they know, and trust.

an organizational kit that will guide you and your neighbors in putting this event together.

Next, begin talking to your neighbors about your idea. Ask them if they would be interested in helping to plan the party. When you find enough interested people, identify a meeting time that works for them. Then send an invitation to the rest of your neighbors, asking them to your house to plan the party.

Instant Intentions

This event provides a great opportunity to involve your small group or church in helping you serve your neighbors. Ask your small group or church members to provide carnival-like games during your event. Your neighbors will be forever grateful for the time to visit with each other as your Christian friends care for their children. These first impressions go a long way in making your neighbors feel comfortable when you invite them to a dinner at your house.

NEIGHBORHOOD PARADE

idea If you live in a neighborhood with lots of young children, a parade will be the perfect neighborhood celebration. Kids love to dress up and show off, and parents love to watch them.

Choose a starting and ending location, either your house or a nearby park, and a starting time. Midmorning or midafternoon would work well. Just make sure you watch the weather for rain showers or extreme heat, and make the appropriate considerations.

Make a map of the parade route, especially if your neighborhood consists of more than one street. Write up a flier inviting the neighborhood to watch and participate in the parade. Be sure to include the map when you hand out the fliers. Your flier should explain that everyone is welcome to participate in the parade. Encourage children to dress up and adults to share any family-friendly talents they have, such as playing an instrument, juggling, or being a clown. Families should be encouraged to make small floats with wagons, strollers, or bikes.

Ask a few volunteers to be the parade conductors, leading the parade through the neighborhood and keeping it moving. The parade conductors can blow whistles to announce the start of the parade. Have participants line up and follow behind the conductors at a slow enough pace that everyone can be seen and little legs will be able to keep up. Have a volunteer or two use digital cameras to take pictures of the children as well as participating adults.

> **HELPFUL HINTS**
> *Create signs for the entrances of your neighborhood stating the time and date of the parade. Hand out whistles, clackers, or other noisemakers and helium balloons to parade participants to liven up the show. Also, make sure parents of small children remain with them during the entire parade. You might ask your local police department to help you block off your street for the hour of the parade.*

Instant Intentions

After you've completed the parade route, gather in someone's yard for refreshments such as ice cream and lemonade. Share digital photos from the parade, relax, and talk. Take the opportunity to get to know a particular person or family, and make plans for a follow-up dinner or lunch together.

PATRIOTIC PET PARADE

idea Here's a patriotic celebration for pet owners. Send out a flier to the neighborhood suggesting a Fourth of July parade for both kids and pets. Especially recommend that kids dress up their pets in patriotic garb and bring along some kind of musical instrument to bang on. Tell them that it will culminate in a picnic on your lawn.

At the specified time, march everyone from one end of the neighborhood to the other. You may pick up a few new recruits along the way!

Fun suggestions might include giving everyone a little flag to wave, printing a participation certificate for everyone who came, or pulling a little wagon with a CD player that plays patriotic music.

Have the parade stop at your house for the picnic at the end. This can always be a potluck to share. You could even suggest that everyone bring food that is either red, white, or blue.

> ### HELPFUL HINTS
> *As an added bonus for everyone, take gifts along for the pets. You could bring a box of dog biscuits or some small chew toys. (A few brushes would be safe for people who have pets on diets!) This is just a way of showing special kindness to the neighborhood.*

Instant Intentions

Of course you can follow up by inviting people to get together in the evening to watch fireworks. But keep the sparklers away from Fido!

Make sure you take lots of pictures during the parade, and offer to have people over to swap them in a week or two.

GO TEAM

SUPER BOWL PARTY

idea Making connections with new neighbors can sometimes be difficult, but using sports as common ground is a sure way to break the ice.

When it comes to football fans, there's no better way to celebrate than with loads of snacks, comfortable seating, and the Super Bowl on TV. Even non-sports fans like to get in on the event. Take advantage of this American pastime by inviting your neighbors to your home on the big day. Get the word out at least two weeks in advance, clear out your TV area so it is primed for extra seating, and pack them in! You may want to ask each person or family to bring a side dish or drink to help offset the cost. You may even get into the spirit of the game by making food color of each NFL team. Remember: Keep the focus of the day on the game. Inviting football fans over to watch the Super Bowl, then talking over it, will leave the wrong impression.

> **HELPFUL HINTS**
>
> *Lots of children in the neighborhood? Screen a movie, or set up games in an adjoining room, and ask a few of the adults to supervise with you. Chances are, several people won't be as avid football fans as others—so take this opportunity to engage in friendly conversation.*

Use the halftime intermission to play an impromptu game of your own. When halftime begins, distribute football cutouts to each guest. Inform your guests that during halftime, they will not be allowed to say the name of either contending team. If a guest hears someone say either team name, he or she can take that person's football cutout. The guest with the most footballs at the end of halftime is the winner.

Instant Intentions

Once you've hosted a Super Bowl party, your neighbors will more than likely be counting on your hospitality for the following year. Seek out the sports enthusiasts attending this event, and utilize this information to open conversations on everything from golf to baseball. You may be inspired to host other sports-related parties throughout the year.

VIBRANT VALENTINE

idea This one is for ladies only! Host a valentine-making party in your home, and get ready to craftily express your love!

Invite the women of your neighborhood to participate in a valentine craft day. Be prepared to provide all of the materials for valentine-making, but don't hesitate to ask others to bring craft items for the group to share. Gather plenty of brightly colored and patterned craft papers, fancy handmade papers, fabric scraps, stickers, craft baubles, candy hearts, pattern-edged scissors, glue, markers, or even a sewing machine for stitching paper or fabric treat pouches (and perhaps some candy to go inside).

Prepare the craft area in your home by covering tables and countertops with protective paper. Scatter the supplies around so they're within easy reach of the crafters. You may want to prepare a couple of valentines as

> **HELPFUL HINTS**
> *Provide a book of elegant verses or love poems for participants to copy onto their valentines. Also, to inspire imagination and creativity, you might set out a book or magazine picturing various crafts.*

examples ahead of time, just to give people a jump-start when they arrive.

Here are some further suggestions for hosting your event:

- Set up an arrangement of light, non-messy refreshments for your guests to enjoy while they're crafting and talking.
- Play a selection of love songs or instrumental music in the background to help set the mood.
- Be sure to facilitate conversation between your guests.
- Don't forget to offer praise and encouragement to your neighbors as their creations emerge.

You could also try adapting this idea to other holidays or even a change in the seasons. Just buy theme-appropriate materials, and provide examples of relevant crafts. For example, for a Christmas craft party you could have guests decorate tree ornaments or create holiday cards.

Instant Intentions

....

Along with the more traditional valentine verses, consider setting out a Bible with pages marked at 1 Corinthians 13 or Ephesians 4:13. You could also mark other fitting Bible passages about love. Be sure to use the Bible yourself to copy some wording onto your valentines. You may be asked about using the Bible verses, so be prepared to briefly explain how these love words from God are meaningful to you in all your relationships.

INDEX

IDEAS GEARED TOWARD KIDS

Autumn Festival	124
Calling All Hands!	20
Community Carnival	23
Easter-Egg Hunt	127
Halloween Alternative	130
Halloween Handouts	131
Helping Kids Excel	29
May Day Baskets	133
National Night Out	135
Neighborhood Baseball	83
Neighborhood Bicycle Exchange	35
Neighborhood Camp Out	84
Neighborhood Parade	137
Neighborhood Splash Day	85
Patriotic Pet Parade	44
Pen Pals and Flower Pots	139
Sledding Social	87
Street Hockey	89

"GUYS ONLY" EVENTS

Eat Meat Club	61
Tournament-Style Fun	118

"JUST FOR LADIES" EVENTS

Christmas Tea	125
Lovely Ladies Tea Party	100
Pamper Yourself Party	115
Vibrant Valentine	141
Women Encouragement Partners	121

Engaging With Culture

All About the Academy Awards   92
Block Book Club   93
Finale Night Party   98
Make the Most of Movie Nights   102
Movie Night   105
Movies 1-6   107-112
Super Bowl Party   140
Weekly Watch   119

Serving Others and Sharing Resources

Bakery Barter Bonanza   52
Calling All Hands!   20
Clothing Exchange   22
Create a Social Pool With a Car Pool   25
Encourage `Em   27
Flower Bulb and Seed Swap   82
Make It Easy to "Do Good"   31
Moving Day   33
Neighborhood Cleanup   36
Neighborhood Vegetable Garden Co-op   86
Neighborhood Watch   40
Pack up the Van   41
Serving Single Parents   46
Swap Meet and Greet   47
Welcome to the Neighborhood   49